"We often think about breaking free from bad habits, past hurts, or negative patterns, but what if the reason we sometimes feel hollow and stuck is because of a subtle but deceptive addiction to 'nice'—acting like we should so we can get what we want. Sharon Hodde Miller's book *Nice* is challenging me and helping me to discover a truer way to live authentically free. Sharon is a refreshing voice full of truth and wisdom."

Lysa TerKeurst, *New York Times* bestselling author
and president of Proverbs 31 Ministries

"As a leader and teacher who prized 'niceness,' I'm shocked by the truth uncovered in *Nice*. It's simple—but true—and completely profound. Niceness has trumped honesty and crept into pulpits, cubicles, and friendships, disguised as a fruit of the Spirit. Sharon bravely prunes and removes the faux virtue and pushes us to bear real fruit."

Bianca Juarez Olthoff, pastor, teacher,
and bestselling author of *Play with Fire*

"'God did not call you to be nice.' Starting with this powerful truth, Sharon unpacks the false idols of our day with humility and passion. She shares how to discern truth and never be locked into the prison of 'nice' again."

Alli Worthington, author of *Fierce Faith*
and founder of The Blissdom Conference

"Our culture is desperate for Jesus's love—his kindness, his compassion, his cross—but we fool ourselves if we think we can replace gospel sacrifice with bland niceness. In these pages, Sharon calls out the spiritual impotence of 'nice Christianity' and invites us into a faith that honors Christ and matters to others. This message is as timely and urgent as ever, which is why I highly recommend this book!"

Dr. Derwin L. Gray, lead pastor of Transformation Church
and author of *Limitless Life*

"I'm passionate about walking in the tension of truth and love, but it's not always easy. Will I choose courage or compromise? Conviction or cliché? Sometimes I slide into the latter easier than I think, all for the sake of being liked. Sharon's new book, *Nice: Why We Love to Be Liked and How God Calls Us to More*, will challenge you to the core to rise up and walk in godly conviction, step into hard conversations, and test the fruit of your life. This book will give you the opportunity to bear rich, authentic, life-giving fruit that lasts."

Andi Andrew, author, speaker, pastor,
and founder of She Is Free

"There is a spirit of venom in our culture today that makes agreeable Christianity seem appealing and benign. Sharon has experienced this temptation in her own life, and she exposes the empty discipleship produced by a faith whose greatest ambition is to be 'nice.' At a time when Christians swing between hair-trigger outrage and shallow likability, this is a vision we need."

Ed Stetzer, Billy Graham Distinguished Chair
at Wheaton College

"As I read Sharon Hodde Miller's new book, *Nice: Why We Love to Be Liked and How God Calls Us to More*, I had two recurring thoughts. The first was—*Oh, my toes*—because Sharon lovingly and convincingly calls out the excuses and the lies that can lurk behind our niceness. The second thought, however, was—*Get it, Sharon Hodde Miller!*—because her words challenge and convict but also call us to be higher and better in our motives, our actions, and our relationships. Beautifully written, thoughtfully structured, and theologically sound, *Nice* will inspire personal reflection and corporate encouragement as we read and ask the Lord to help us be who we say we are and who he calls us to be."

Sophie Hudson, author of *Giddy Up* and *Eunice* and cohost of *The Big Boo Cast*

"The title of this book, *Nice: Why We Love to Be Liked and How God Calls Us to More*, may evoke feelings of soft, sweet Christian living, but author Sharon Hodde Miller tackles the topic of motivation and acceptance with scholarly depth and substance. Sharon skillfully guides readers to understand how our emphasis on being 'nice' misses God's greater purposes of spiritual maturity and genuine transformation. Challenging and needed during this age of polarization in our nation and shallow social media soundbites, I am grateful for Sharon's example, heart, and timely message found in the pages of this book."

Vivian Mabuni, speaker and author of *Open Hands, Willing Heart*

"As an outspoken, justice-driven woman who has struggled with the word *nice* my whole life, I needed to read this book. Sharon Hodde Miller not only helped me wisely sort through the truth about my struggles, but she also reminded me of my gospel responsibility to choose Jesus over myself. I find *Nice* a must-read for every believer maneuvering the difficult road of human opinion—I dare say, a struggle for us all."

Lisa Whittle, author of 5 *Word Prayers* and *I Want God*, Bible teacher, and podcast host of *Jesus Over Everything*

"The soul-crushing desire to be liked and accepted can manifest itself in many ways. For Sharon Hodde Miller, it was through an idol we won't likely consider on our own—the idol of niceness. In her book *Nice*, Miller turns our accepted notions of niceness on their heads, challenging us to think of a better, more biblical way to engage the world and others and root out sin that keeps us from true and honest virtues. God can turn our niceness and self-focus to a grace-filled love for others, and I believe this book is a helpful tool he could use along the journey."

Trillia Newbell, author of *If God Is For Us*, *Fear and Faith*, and *God's Very Good Idea*

"Sharon is the ideal person from whom to learn to let go of the need to be liked. I've watched her over the years and have longed to know her secrets. Sharon possesses the ability to be kind but rejects the temptation to stop at being 'nice.' She is a fierce voice for truth. When we let go of being liked, we grow in the unique way God made us, the passions he put in our hearts and, most of all, the integrity he instilled in us. I'm grateful to have Sharon as an example and a teacher."

Hayley Morgan, author of *Preach to Yourself* and coauthor of *Wild and Free*

NICE

WHY WE LOVE TO BE LIKED AND
HOW GOD CALLS US TO MORE

Sharon Hodde Miller

BakerBooks

a division of Baker Publishing Group
Grand Rapids, Michigan

Published by Baker Books
a division of Baker Publishing Group
PO Box 6287, Grand Rapids, MI 49516-6287
www.bakerbooks.com

Printed in the United States of America

Library of Congress Cataloging-in-Publication Data
Names: Miller, Sharon Hodde, 1981- author.
Title: Nice : why we love to be liked and how God calls us to more / Sharon Hodde
    Miller.
Description: Grand Rapids : Baker Books, a division of Baker Publishing Group,
    2019. |
Identifiers: LCCN 2019002814 | ISBN 9780801075247 (pbk.)
Subjects: LCSH: Self-esteem—Religious aspects—Christianity. | Self-acceptance—
    Religious aspects—Christianity. | Fruit of the Spirit. | Social acceptance. |
    Integrity—Religious aspects—Christianity.
Classification: LCC BV4598.24 .M55 2019 | DDC 248.4—dc23
LC record available at https://lccn.loc.gov/2019002814

In keeping with biblical principles of creation stewardship, Baker Publishing Group advocates the responsible use of our natural resources. As a member of the Green Press Initiative, our company uses recycled paper when possible. The text paper of this book is composed in part of post-consumer waste.

19 20 21 22 23 24 25   7 6 5 4 3 2 1

To my Sadie girl.
You burst into our lives as I crafted these words
about courage, character, and conviction.
I pray that, one day, you will grow into a woman who bears
these good fruits, but my greatest hope for you is this:
That you would know how wildly you are loved
by us and by your Father in heaven.
We are so glad you are here.

CONTENTS

INTRODUCTION

God did not call you to be nice.

This statement has been rattling around in my head for well over a year now, and I haven't been able to shake it. It has re-emerged at crucial moments, not as an excuse to be snarky, angry, or rude, but because I have noticed something going on in my heart, and in the church, for a while now: A competing allegiance. A warm and inviting idolatry that has managed to wedge itself between us and true obedience to Christ.

In my first book, *Free of Me*, I began the work of understanding this spiritual stronghold, which doesn't sound like a stronghold at all. In that book, I described my identity as a "nice Christian girl." For as long as I can remember, I have loved to be nice—not just loved but *needed*—and it is an identity I have struggled to leave behind. Even now, while writing this book, I have squirmed and deleted and rewritten and repeated because I was afraid of how my words would come across. I don't want to be scary or intimidating or unlikable. I want to be accepted, and I want to be embraced.

And so, to this day, my idol of choice is a very pretty one.

I identify "niceness" as an idol in my life because I have served it tirelessly, and it has served me well in return. In our culture, niceness is not just a socially acceptable behavior but an openly encouraged one. The world gushes over nice Christians, and for obvious reasons. Nice Christians follow the rules. Nice Christian kids obey their parents. Nice Christian employees are dependable. Nice Christian neighbors aren't too loud. Nice Christian students do their homework. And nice Christian church members always show up, always do what they are asked, and always do it with a smile.

The rewards are many for being nice. Parents love it. Grandparents praise it. Teachers reward it. Pastors celebrate it. And so, as a nice Christian girl, I settled into that identity comfortably. Throughout my childhood I played by the rules. I people-pleased. I made good grades. I went to church every week. "Nice Christian girl" was what I did, but it was also who I was. The highest priority in my heart, just a step above following Jesus, was my *reputation* as a girl who followed Jesus.

I probably wouldn't have articulated it so shrewdly at the time, but on some level I understood that niceness *gets* you things. It earned me a lot of attention and positive affirmation, and because of this, it wasn't long before my motives for being nice became extremely muddled. I was a nice kid, not simply for Jesus's sake but also for my own.

Ever since I first wrote about this part of my childhood, I knew I wasn't done with it. I knew this topic deserved more than a few paragraphs, because I can see its wide-ranging effects in my life. My devotion to niceness has won me a lot of acceptance and praise, but it has also inhibited my courage, fed my self-righteousness, encouraged my inauthenticity, and produced in me a flimsy sweetness that easily gives way to disdain.

Once I noticed these yawning gaps in my spiritual growth, I knew I needed to dig deeper to understand their relationship to niceness, but I felt burdened to explore them for other reasons as well. In addition to noticing the stronghold of niceness in my life, I noticed it in others: The community shocked by their neighbor's secret life because she was "just so nice." The leader forgiven of his moral failure because he is incredibly nice. The family falling apart at the seams, while maintaining an image of "perfect niceness" online.

There was also the daily usefulness of niceness. It has become a social currency in our culture, one that we value highly without ever really realizing it. I once discussed this topic with Dr. Christina Edmondson, dean of intercultural student development at Calvin College and cohost of the podcast "Truth's Table," and she remarked that "we are wooed by superficial niceness. Satiated by it." We will forgive all manner of ills in a person we deem to be nice. We use niceness to grease the wheels of our social interactions. We employ niceness like a ladder, helping us to scale the heights of our career. We smuggle white lies inside the Trojan Horse of niceness for the sake of preserving relationships. And for many Christians, following Jesus means we are just really, *really* nice. All of this alerted me to the supreme value of niceness in our culture. Niceness is not merely a pleasant trait, it is a trump card. It has tremendous social power, so much so that it can overshadow virtually any vice.

That was my second reason for returning to this topic. The third reason, the thing that convinced me niceness is not just a social skill but a competing priority in our lives, was watching how the world responds to people who stray outside the expectations of niceness, as if they have violated some holy, unspoken social contract. The friend who says a hard thing that we need to hear, the pastor who holds us accountable, the leader who disrupts the status quo—these not-nice behaviors are frequently met with swift rejection and even rage. Friendships end. Church members leave. Social media burns with outrage. These kinds of reactions tell us something about the role of niceness in our culture. Niceness, I realized, is not just a social expectation; it's a sacred cow.

Now let me take a second to make this clear. Christians are, without exception, called to kindness, gentleness, and love. I am not advocating for harshness, meanness, mudslinging, or name-calling that passes itself off as "courageous" or "bold." Instead, I am talking about the price we pay when we stray outside the bounds of "pleasant" or "encouraging" to say something "timely" and "true." Even when we are winsome, careful, and abounding in grace, there is a cost to speaking truth that isn't "nice." Especially when that truth impinges on the culture's idols or the idols that are present in our own communities.

As a lifelong nice girl, I have not only felt this pressure but I have also caved in to it often. The need to be nice has influenced my ministry as well as my relationships. I have backed away from hard conversations or softened my convictions, opting instead for the wide gate of niceness.

But after doing this for years and observing the fruit of this false idol in my life, here is what I have concluded: I cannot follow Jesus and nice. Not equally. Because following Jesus means following a man who spoke hard and confusing truths, who was honest with his disciples—even when it hurt—who condemned the hypocrisy of the Pharisees and turned over tables in the temple. Jesus was a man who went face-to-face with the devil himself and died on a cross rather than succumb to the status quo. Jesus was loving. He was gracious. He was forgiving. He was kind. But he was not nice. He was a man who would leave the ninety-nine sheep to rescue the one, but he was also totally unafraid of offending people.

Jesus understood the difference between graciousness and personal compromise, between speaking truth and needlessly alienating people. Rather than wear a shiny veneer, he became the embodiment of rugged love.

This, not niceness, is what we are called to. But it's not quite as simple as that. We exist in a world that swings between sweetness and outrage, two behaviors that seem to be at odds with one another. In reality, they are two sides of the same coin: a lack of spiritual formation. When our civility isn't rooted in something sturdy and deep, when our good behavior isn't springing from the core of who we are but is instead merely a mask we put on, it is only a matter of time before the façade crumbles away and our true state is revealed: an entire generation of people who are really good at looking good.

The solution, then, is not to trade in our appearance of niceness for an appearance of boldness. We have to go deeper. We have to cultivate something entirely new.

The Fruit Is Bad

In Matthew 7, Jesus uses an analogy I will draw on throughout this book. Describing false teachers, he warns:

> You will recognize them by their fruits. Are grapes gathered from thornbushes, or figs from thistles? So, **every healthy tree bears good fruit, but the diseased tree bears bad fruit.** A healthy tree cannot bear bad fruit, nor can a diseased tree bear good fruit. Every tree that does not bear good fruit is cut down and thrown into the fire. Thus you will recognize them by their fruits. (vv. 16–20, emphasis added)

Although this passage refers to the specific context of false teaching, it derives from a universal principle—**bad trees produce bad fruit.** With this principle in mind, the first half of this book will identify the bad fruits of niceness. We are starting with the fruits instead of the root for the same reason Jesus did—it's how we recognize the tree. This first section will not only identify unhealthy fruits you may have missed or simply denied but it will also serve as a personal health check. Call it a heart diagnosis. If you spot any of these fruits in your life, it could be a sign of your own excessive commitment to niceness.

Once we identify the bad fruits of niceness, we will spend the second half of the book looking at how to cultivate a better tree, including practical steps to guide your way and produce real and lasting change.

◊ ◊ ◊ ◊ ◊ ◊ ◊

With all that's going on in the world, niceness might seem like a minor problem. But this idol is only small in the way that aphids are small. These insects cause mostly superficial damage by ingesting a plant's sap; however, they can cause serious, if not fatal, harm through the transmission of viruses that kill. Niceness is like that. Its immediate impact seems trivial—people-pleasing, brownnosing, pretending to like a present you hate—but when it becomes a habit of our lives and our faith, its fruit is bad and its long-term harvest is barren.

This particular problem—letting niceness become a habit—is what we are going to focus on. This means two things: First, this book is not a takedown of all niceness. Niceness is not wrong or inherently bad. My aim is not to villainize nice people or banish the word from our lexicon. Instead, niceness is like any good or neutral thing, which becomes a broken thing when it becomes an ultimate thing.[1] When we turn to niceness for peace in our relationships, promotions in our workplace, preference in our community, and power in our ministry, niceness is no longer a harmless social default but an alternative god whose promises compete with Christ.

What I want to do in these pages is consider how we have made niceness into an ultimate thing, how we use niceness to get what we want, what that is doing to our spiritual lives, and how it's undermining our credibility in the world.

Second—and I cannot say this enough—this book is not a defense of rudeness, anger, malice, meanness, or aggression. I am not advocating that we say whatever we feel and "let the chips fall where they may." These are fruits of a different tree that also needs to be pruned.

Niceness is a characteristic that most of us love to use, but it can end up using us instead. It becomes a master we fear to defy, and as a result, it eventually stands between us and obedience. What each of us needs in place of the superficial virtue of niceness is a soul rooted and abiding in Christ. We need to be transformed so fully and completely that we actually are who we present ourselves to be. We need to cultivate a fruit that, instead of tasting worse than it looks, tastes even *better* than we could imagine.

To that end, each chapter will conclude with two practical steps: a passage of Scripture to meditate on or memorize and reflection questions. I have titled the first section "Taking Root," because we root ourselves in the Word of God when we write his Scripture on our hearts. The second I have called "Digging Deeper," because this is a dirt-under-your-fingernails endeavor.

So let's roll up our sleeves and get to the work of pruning this habit from our lives and this idol from our hearts. Ecclesiastes 3:2 (NIV) says, "[There is] a time to plant and a time to uproot," and I believe we need a season of uprooting. So here I am, raising an ax, and inviting you to join me.

The Fruit of Niceness

Every year at the end of November, my husband, Ike, and I load the kids in the car and drive to the nearest Christmas tree lot. We are committed "real tree" people—not to be confused with "fake tree" people who keep their trees stored in a box—so the hunt for the perfect tree is one we anticipate and enjoy every year. No matter where we live or how busy we are, we set aside time to visit a farm or a store in order to make our pick. Ike, the kids, and I painstakingly inspect every single option, examine them for gaps, assess their sizes, and scan for brown spots. Then, after we have made our choice, Ike hoists the tree on top of our car, ties it down, and drives us home.

Once we get back to the house, we carefully mount the tree on the stand and carry it inside, trying to scatter as few needles as possible. For the rest of the night, the sap on our fingers attracts dirt, hair, fuzz, and other light debris. I don't like the mess and I don't like the hassle, but it's a hassle we are happy to endure. Nothing beats the smell of Fraser fir filling the air, and nothing transports Ike and me to our childhood Christmases quite like the glow of a fresh tree in our home.

At least, that is how it normally goes. Several years ago our Norman Rockwell moment was not to be. Ike and I bought a discount tree at a local store. That was probably our first mistake. The tree had several bald patches and multiple brown spots. The branches were dry and the needles prickly. We should have read the signs, but I was optimistic. I thought I could hide the gaps with some faux poinsettias and no one would be the wiser. So we took the tree home.

For the first few days, the tree was stunning. I loaded it with ornaments, ribbons, and pearls. It was shiny, full, and smelled like an evergreen forest. It was probably the most aromatic tree we've ever had. All was well except for one niggling concern: the tree wasn't taking any water.

If you have ever purchased a real tree, you know they guzzle water, especially at first, and especially after the lights have been weighing on their branches for a while. But not this one. Every time I checked the stand, the water level had barely dropped. That's when I suspected something wasn't quite right.

Not long after, the branches were drying out, and the needles became so thorny I flinched to brush against them. And the smell that I loved so much? Over time the scent of evergreen was replaced with a musty, rotten odor. That was when it became clear: our tree wasn't just a dud. Our tree was dead.

That was a disappointing year in the Miller home. We decided to keep the tree for those remaining days before Christmas, but whenever I passed by it, I was reminded of something

I had missed amid all the Christmases before. No matter how much you dress up a "real tree," no matter how much you cover it in family heirlooms, silver bells, tinsel, and lights, a Christmas tree is still a dying tree.

And this, I realized, was a tree-shaped sermon about my life.

Good at Looking Good

Christianity can be such a pretty faith. God calls us to wonderful things, to noble deeds, and to be a people of love. We are meant to be kind, joyful, brave, and good. These are attractive qualities that most people would love to be known for, Christian or not.

The trouble is, we can approach the Christian life in the same way we decorate a Christmas tree, by piling on pleasing spiritual adornments. We can dress up our lives with church commitments, community service, spiritual language, a clean-cut family, and an upbeat attitude. All of these things look so great—so *Christian*—while obscuring what is really going on underneath. Beneath all the spiritual glitz, we can exist cut off from our root system, without detection. We can appear to be thriving, even though we are disconnected from the vine.

Many of us are masters at this. We look great on the outside while withering on the inside. It's easy to pull off this illusion because humans are a lot like the evergreen trees we display in our homes. We can maintain the appearance of flourishing long after we have uprooted our souls. My neighbor once tossed her Christmas tree into the woods in her backyard, and it was weeks before the tree showed any sign of decay. Weeks! The

21

human soul is like that. Our spiritual decay can take months, even years, to make itself known. We can conceal our dead spots for long periods of time, appearing healthy, vibrant, and thriving at the same time that we are dying. But we can't hide the sickness forever. As radiant as my tree appeared, the decorations couldn't mask the smell. And neither can we. We can only maintain the illusion for so long before reality begins to poke through.

For many of us, that Christmas tree is our story. We look great, our church looks great, everything seems fine. Until the day we pull back the branches and discover the sickness hiding within. Underneath all the ministry commitments, the Christian conferences, the growing churches, the bestselling books, and the uplifting social media posts, there is fear. There is pride. There is a need to control. There is self-preservation in place of generosity. Defensiveness in place of humility. Silence in place of boldness. Shouting in place of listening. Cynicism in place of hope. We can hide all of these things behind the ornaments of nice Christianity, which allows them to exist undetected for years.

These ornaments do not simply mask the sickness, they contribute to it as well. The baubles that decorate brittle branches also weigh them down. The lights that obscure a tree's dehydration dry it out faster. Niceness does the same. Our need to be nice, our need to be liked, our commitment to the appearance of being a certain kind of Christian all become a burden that our increasingly weary souls must bear. Abiding in niceness instead of abiding in Christ wilts our souls at the same time it gives us the appearance of life.

So, how did we get here? What is it about being nice that we love so much? The word *nice* generally means "pleasant, agreeable, delightful,"[1] but for the purposes of this book, I want to define the idol of niceness very specifically. The idol of niceness refers to the ways we make ourselves pleasant, agreeable, acceptable, or likable **in order to get something.** We use niceness to achieve belonging or avoid conflict, but we also use it to amass influence and power. We use niceness to succeed in the workplace or to manage the way people perceive us. Niceness has incredible weight in our culture—both inside and outside the church—and although few of us would admit to using it so slickly (and we maybe haven't been aware that we are until now), many of us do. Niceness motivates us, reassures us, and promises greater ease in our social interactions. It is also the reason our message is uncompelling and our witness limp. Niceness is a false form of spiritual formation that has crept into the church, seduced Jesus's followers, and taken much of the power out of our lives. It is one of our generation's favorite idols, and it is high past time to name it.

A Short History of Niceness

I don't think it is an overstatement to say that niceness has a hold on us, but in order to understand why that is, it helps to understand how it came to be.

Like many words, *nice* has meant different things at different times. Its meaning has evolved throughout the centuries, dating as far back as 1604 when the word *nice* was featured in the first dictionary of the English language, Robert Cawdrey's *A Table*

Alphabeticall. There it is defined as "'slow and laysie,' and its origins are deemed unequivocally French."[2]

In her book *American Niceness*, author Carrie Tirado Bramen explains that early on, nice had a variety of meanings. In the sixteenth and seventeenth centuries, nice was "an ambiguous term that could be either an insult or a compliment, referring to someone who was either ostentatiously or elegantly dressed."[3] However, by the early 1800s, its meaning had shifted again to simply mean pleasing.[4]

In addition to this positive definition, nice has also carried with it a connotation of *silence*. In her book *The Tyranny of Niceness*, psychologist Evelyn Sommers traces the word back to its Latin roots and shares this insight.

> When we fail to express our thoughts and opinions or refuse to hear what others say . . . There is a shutting down—or silencing—of oneself or the other. In this way, silence, in some form or degree, is the essential characteristic of being nice.[5]

Without getting too abstract, I think this is a really fascinating way of describing niceness. **Niceness is not necessarily what you *do*** (being kind, showing love, acting generously) **but what you *don't*** do (not speaking your mind, not saying hard things, not challenging injustice). In short, nice is the social equivalent of wallpaper. It's dressing up the walls without providing any furniture to sit on.

Even so, our culture gives niceness a tremendous amount of weight. Almost illogically so. I can't imagine walking into a house and declaring, "The roof is leaking and the foundation is crumbling but the *wallpaper*! I'll take it!" And yet that is the kind of priority we give to niceness. That is how greatly we value it in our social interactions and how we assess other people: Were they *nice*? And more specifically: Were they nice to *me*?

The prioritization of niceness takes two distinct forms: one in our broader culture and one in the church. In our broader culture, niceness is a **false virtue**, and in the church it is a **false idol**. Let's begin with the first.

False Virtue

Going back to ancient times, *virtue* has traditionally referred to a particular moral good. In Plato's *Republic*, the philosopher names four classical virtues: wisdom, temperance, courage, and justice. These virtues are not merely about doing the right thing but the *why* behind it. Plato describes virtue as "the desire of things honorable,"[6] which means we are motivated by a greater good outside ourselves.

Niceness, on the other hand, aims small. Bramen describes niceness as a virtue of "surfaces rather than depths,"[7] while Philip Ryken, president of Wheaton College, calls it "a trivial virtue that is easy to fake."[8] Niceness is concerned with the appearance of goodness, not the reality of it. In fact, niceness doesn't tell us much about reality at all.

Unfortunately the deceptive nature of niceness hasn't stopped us from relying on it for information. Instead we depend on niceness to assess a person's character. For this reason, Bramen describes niceness as a "permanent get-out-of-jail-free card" that exempts people "from acknowledging the consequences of their actions."[9] In our culture, niceness covers over a multitude of sins.

On some level, we all know this about niceness, which is why theologian Miroslav Volf describes niceness as a "social lubricant."[10] We commonly utilize niceness to navigate conflict and facilitate relationships, and we do this because niceness gets us what we want. Sommers writes,

> We believe that being nice will ease the beginning of relationships, endear us to people, hold relationships together, prevent emotional pain for ourselves and others, cover up our flaws or unkind thoughts, mask our true motives, spare us from having to say things that are hard to say, and provide us with a peaceful existence.[11]

Sommers is highlighting something about niceness that I don't want you to miss. We typically assume niceness is about a deep-seated need to be liked and gain approval. Sometimes that is true, but it's only the tip of the iceberg. More broadly, we are nice because it is to our benefit to be. Niceness gets us something we want, whether that is approval, influence, power, inclusion, or closing a deal. Belonging is only one of many prizes we use niceness to win.

Niceness has the appearance of serving others but it exists primarily to serve ourselves, and that is why niceness is a *false virtue*. Both Plato and his contemporary, Aristotle, believed that virtue is oriented toward a bigger vision. It is tied to "humanity's ultimate end or purpose."[12] Christians would later adapt this view and direct it toward Christ, meaning that true Christian virtue points us, and others, to God.

Niceness only pretends to do this, but it can pretend rather convincingly. We can put on a good exterior "for Jesus," but this is not the same as true virtue. Virtue is not about appearance but motivation. It's not about how we look but who we are becoming. Unlike false virtue, true virtue can never be unmasked. It is what it appears to be, and this is what we should long for and pray for in ourselves. The false virtue of niceness only makes us into "whitewashed tombs" (Matt. 23:27), pristine on the outside but empty within.

False Idol

In addition to being a false virtue, niceness is also a false idol. In order to better understand what that means, I want to explain idolatry in a slightly different way than you may have heard before.

Since the beginning of creation, humans have struggled to fully trust God. We have always had a backup, a Plan B in case God didn't come through. At the first sign of delay, the first worry that God might not show up, we run to our backup plan for help, and that backup plan is called an idol.

The irony, of course, is that the backup plan is the true intention of your heart. It's what you really trust to come through for you. It's what you *actually* depend on to give you what you want, regardless of what you say. Thousands of years ago, these backup plans took the form of alternative religions. If your crops needed rain, you turned to the god of rain for help. If you needed to win a battle, you turned to the god of war. If you wanted to have children, you turned to the goddess of fertility.

In the centuries since, our backups have changed but human nature has not. Our idols have shifted away from mythical characters and evolved into full-blown lifestyles. Financial security, professional success, academic performance, physical appearance—each one offers itself as an appealing backup plan for attaining peace, provision, and joy, just in case God doesn't come through with it himself.

Niceness offers itself as an attractive backup plan. It promises conflict-free relationships, acceptance, praise, and influence. These are rewards that honesty, transparency, and obedience to God do not guarantee. And so, when it comes to marriage, friendship, and social networking, niceness becomes our provider of choice.

However, Christians sometimes take this a step further. As I mentioned earlier, when I was growing up "niceness" became a part of my faith. I assumed that being a good Christian meant being a nice, likable person, so I conflated the two. I strove to be liked, whether it pointed people to Jesus or not. I made the mistake that author Randy Alcorn describes this way: "We've been schooled that it's inappropriate to say anything negative. Being a good witness once meant faithfully representing Christ, even when it meant being unpopular. Now it means 'making people like us.' We've redefined *Christlike* to mean 'nice.'"[13]

Not surprisingly, this false idol has shaped the reputation of Christians throughout the world. Alcorn explains, "Many non-believers know only two kinds of Christians: those who speak truth without grace and those who are very nice but never share the truth."[14]

In my own life, I noticed myself sliding toward the latter. When confronted with hypocrisy or injustice among fellow Christians, I hemmed and hawed over whether to speak up. What if people got mad? What if people called me names? What if people questioned my motives? Similarly, I was timid with friends who were making destructive decisions. My need to be liked undermined the value of speaking truth and, ultimately, loving them.

And so, too often I went with my backup plan. I selected the option that caused the least amount of waves, the option that didn't require hard conversations and didn't risk any loss. I followed a version of Christianity that actually led me further from Christ.

The Two Aims of Niceness

Because niceness is both a false virtue in the world and a false idol in the church, it shapes our lives in two distinct yet overlapping ways: the desire to be a nice *person* and the desire to be a nice *Christian*. The desire to be a nice person is nearly universal. Regardless of faith, most of us yearn to be accepted and liked, and this desire produces a variety of fruits in our lives, which we will explore in the following chapters. These fruits look healthy and sweet on the outside, but inside they have spoiled. When you take a bite into these fruits and really taste them, you discover the **fake** fruit of inauthenticity, the **rotten** fruit of corruption, the **bitter** fruit of cynicism, and the **bland** fruit of cowardice.

In addition to those four fruits, there is a religious form of niceness that is focused on being a nice Christian. Its two fruits are a little more specific than the others, because they are oriented toward being a nice *Christian*. Like the other fruits, these look good on the outside, but when you bite into them, you discover the **hard** fruit of self-righteousness and the **processed** fruit of sentimentality.

I hope the following chapters will feel a bit like pulling back the branches, peering behind the ornaments, and assessing the health of your tree. And I hope what you discover will instill in you a holy urgency. Not guilt but gumption, because this matters. Our spiritual health and our spiritual fruit *matter*. It's how people know who we are, but more importantly, it's how people know who we follow.

TAKING ROOT

I am the vine, you are the branches; he who abides in Me and I in him, he bears much fruit, for apart from Me you can do nothing. (John 15:5 NASB)

DIGGING DEEPER

1. What did you learn about niceness that you never knew or had never thought about before?
2. Looking at your own life, in what ways have you used niceness to get things?

3. In what ways have you seen niceness take the form of a false virtue in the world?

4. In what ways have you seen niceness take the form of a false idol in the church?

2

Fake

THE FRUIT OF INAUTHENTICITY

Just to the right of our fireplace sits a tall, dark cabinet full of long-stem wineglasses and gold-laced china we have never used a day in our lives. Each of these breakables sits safely out of the reach of tiny, prying fingers, while sturdier items, like a reclaimed wood silverware caddy and a faux ivy plant, occupy the lower shelves. On top of the cabinet sits a potted lily, a photo of our family, and an old, rusted milk jug.

Of all the items displayed on the cabinet—the china, the glasses, the family photo—the thing I love most is the milk jug. I'm not entirely sure how old it is—fifty years, at least—but it's an artifact of my mother-in-law's family farm. For generations now, the Teagues have been dairy farmers. Nestled in the hills of Elon, North Carolina, Reedy Fork Farm remains a hub of my husband's extended family. Whenever we visit them, we trek through endless fields speckled with grazing cows and goats, and it feels like traveling back to an era when families lived and worked the land together. It feels that way because that is precisely what my mother-in-law's family still does. For decades her entire family has lived on or adjacent to that farm. To this day her parents still live in the same brick ranch in which she grew up, overlooking barns, a chicken coop, and rolling green hills.

Over the years the farm has evolved with the changing times. The cows are now milked by machine, and the family transitioned to organic nearly ten years ago. Despite these changes, the grounds are still dotted with remnants of the past: a broken-down tractor blanketed in kudzu, a barn so dilapidated you can see straight through it, and old milk jugs of every shape and size.

The jug that sits in our home is about ten inches high. It's tiny as far as milk jugs go, probably a half-gallon size. The finish is brown with worn edges where the silver tin pokes through. There is nothing particularly special about it, but it tells the story of my husband's family and gives our home a feeling of rootedness.

It's also the only true antique in our house. Like many American homes today, ours is filled with distressed, old-fashioned-looking furniture. There's my reclaimed wood farm table, the rustic window frame hanging on our wall, and the rusted lantern that sits on our mantle. My house is full of these quaint vintage touches, as if I pillaged a flea market nearby.

But with the exception of the milk jug, all of it is fake. The window frame was never actually a window. The lantern was never meant to be lit. I don't even know if my reclaimed table is made of genuine reclaimed wood. This style looks authentic, but none of it is real. The only antique with any real history is that tiny milk jug.

The Trend of Authenticity

When I first considered the casualties of niceness, I realized "authenticity" was a big one, but I also hesitated to write about it. Authenticity is popular right now, to the point of being cliché. Church after church promotes authenticity as a value. Leaders and authors strive to be authentic in their work, and social media influencers attract followers based on how "real" they are.

But the popularity of authenticity is precisely why it remains so evasive. The mass craving for authenticity drives all sorts of consumer products and experiences, ranging from distressed jeans with pretorn knee holes to advertising gimmicks like the Dove campaign for beauty, which is designed to seem "real" while selling you something. Author Andy Crouch noticed this trend at a Cracker Barrel restaurant, which he described as "a homey, weathered place where a welcoming fire emanates from gas nozzles. On the walls at Cracker Barrel hang nearly 1,000 pieces of Americana, lovingly collected and restored to a suitably worn appearance. Each one has a bar code."[1]

These fake antiques—both at Cracker Barrel and in my house—are a reminder that authenticity sells. In fact, you can read several books with titles that admit as much: *Authenticity: What Consumers Really Want* and *Authenticity: The Head, Heart, and Soul of Selling*. In his book *Pour Your Heart Into It: How Starbucks Built a Company One Cup at a Time*, Starbucks CEO Howard Schultz writes, "Mass advertising can help build brands, but authenticity is what makes them last. If people believe they share values with a company, they will stay loyal to the brand."[2] In other words, authenticity is good business. Christians seem to think so too. The Christian version of fake authenticity is *strategic vulnerability*. It's the mommy blogger who describes her messy life of overflowing laundry and wild kids. It's the pastor who wants you to know he's one of the guys because he drinks beer. Christian authenticity often takes the form of low-stakes confessions or a concerted effort to appear down-to-earth, all with the goal of seeming relatable.

Generally speaking, I think these strategies are well-intentioned, but I can't help but wonder if authenticity—true authenticity—has gotten lost. That's why I almost skipped this chapter. Authenticity itself has become so fashionable that it's now a tool for manipulating people, something you perform in order to get what you want. As Crouch put it, "Our longing for 'authenticity' . . . bears a suspicious resemblance to the latest plot twist in the story of consumer culture: the tendency to rapidly replace the squeaky-clean franchise with the 'authentic' franchise."[3] Both inside and outside the church, we have turned authenticity into a product, which has had the ironic effect of making authenticity inauthentic.

Even so, I knew I had to include this chapter for two reasons. The first is that we do, in fact, crave the real. Our souls flourish in the truth and wither under the false. Scripture affirms this again and again. It's why Jesus describes himself as "the truth" (John 14:6), why the Bible is described as "the word of truth" (James 1:18), and why Jesus promises that "the truth will set you free" (John 8:32). If "authenticity" refers to what is real and what is true, then authenticity is much more than a trend. Inasmuch as God gets to define "real" and "true," authenticity is something we should aspire to.

The second reason I included this topic is that niceness has a way of seeming authentic in the same way my fake antiques seem authentic. Niceness, like my farm table, has the appearance of something real. It resembles intimacy, or healthy relationships, or character without having to commit to the reality of those things. As Brennan Manning once put it, "The temptation of the age is to look good without being good."[4] Niceness tries its darndest to look authentically good, but it's a fake. That is why we are starting with the fake fruit of inauthenticity. Niceness is a deceptive fruit that makes space for other bad fruits to grow. In this way, inauthenticity is both a fertilizer and a fruit, and it takes three primary forms in our lives.

False Kindness

Call it the "*American Idol* Effect." During the early auditions of every season, viewers are treated to a handful of royal messes. It's not just that they sing badly. It's not just that they're "pitchy." It's that they have absolutely no idea. They are frothing with confidence, possessing a concrete certainty that this is their moment to shine.

But we know how this goes. Each of these naïve, starry-eyed contestants walks into the room, stands before the judges, and opens their mouth. And that's when all of America watches and wonders, *How?*

How did they make it this far without anyone telling them the truth? How did they wind up on national television without a single family member sitting them down for an honest conversation? Did all of their friends conspire to uphold this deception? Doesn't anyone love them enough to tell them the truth?

A part of me always wonders if the contestants are truly that oblivious. Some people are happy to grab their fifteen minutes of fame, no matter the cost. And yet the *American Idol* Effect isn't new. In the early 1900s, New York socialite Florence Foster Jenkins became famous for her awful voice. A lifelong patron of the opera, Jenkins herself loved to sing, and in her seventies she began offering private performances, which is where she developed her infamous reputation. Her singing was so bad that critics delighted in finding just the right words to capture its dreadfulness. One of my favorite descriptions came from a contemporary writer who described Jenkins as charging "at the repertoire's most challenging arias like a blind, braying, three-legged horse in a steeplechase, rarely clearing a musical hurdle."[5]

In 2016 Meryl Streep played Jenkins in a movie about the singer's life. The film portrays Jenkins as ignorant both to the quality of her voice and the ridicule of others. In real life it remains unclear what Jenkins understood. Her audience—largely composed of her patrons—applauded and supported her, but one can't shake the feeling that the people "protecting" her feelings were, in reality, humiliating her.

These stories are extreme examples of the false kindness of niceness. It wears the veneer of kindness, but it is not truly loving. In fact, its outcome can be cruel. When we shield people from the truth—not because we are trying to be fake or because we enjoy lying to people—our niceness can *feel* loving, even when it's not.

This is how niceness devolves into falsity. To some extent, it begins with a good and loving desire. Oftentimes we choose niceness instead of truthfulness because we don't want to hurt people. We want to lift them up and encourage them. And a part of me wants to honor and appreciate that desire, because our world needs as much goodwill as it can get. But this also begs the question: What is the difference between niceness—which appears nowhere in the Bible—and godly, truthful *kindness*?

In her book *On Reading Well*, author Karen Swallow Prior teases this difference out, clarifying that the word "*kind* comes from the same root from which we get the word *kin*. To be kind, then, is to treat someone like they are family."[6] Granted, not all families exemplify this ideal (hence the *American Idol* Effect), but in his book, *Love Kindness*, president of Biola University Barry H. Corey offers an additional perspective to distinguish the two. He writes, "Whereas aggression has a firm center and hard edges, niceness has soft edges and a spongy center. Niceness may be pleasant, but it lacks conviction. It has no soul. Niceness trims its sails to prevailing cultural winds and wanders aimlessly, standing for nothing and thereby falling for everything."[7] This "spongy center" is what makes niceness so malleable. It's like a ship without an anchor. There is nothing that keeps it fixed and in place, so it drifts with the circumstances.

Kindness, on the other hand, has "a firm center with soft edges."[8] Kindness has conviction. It has courage. It has a solid backbone. It's also after something more than being accepted or getting along. Author Emily Freeman describes kindness as "a warm meal, a soft word, a high five, an offer to help, and an unwavering willingness to be rejected."[9] Similarly, Philip Ryken defines kindness as "a radical commitment that calls every follower of Christ to costly love."[10] In other words, kindness is not blandly pleasant, and it's definitely not safe. Kindness takes risk. It walks lovingly toward difficulty and even derision. It does not shrink in the face of conflict. Niceness avoids, avoids, avoids. It retreats from the prospect of adversity, preferring instead the comfort of the status quo. Kindness doesn't revel in tumult, but it does have the fortitude to persevere in love in spite of it.

Kindness and niceness are easy to confuse, because they both have the "soft edges" that welcome others and facilitate social interactions. One way to distinguish them is knowing who they aim to please. One is motivated by people-pleasing, the other by faithfulness to God. And what the stories of Florence Foster Jenkins and the *American Idol* contestants remind us is that people-pleasing eventually fails on both fronts. Evelyn Sommers explains, "Although niceness is often intended to bridge difficult relationship problems and smooth over troubling issues, more often it creates fissures and leaves people feeling hurt and alienated."[11] When people-pleasing is our guide, we will fail to love God or others well. This is an outcome Corey pinpoints in his book: "Niceness is keeping an employee in the job, knowing he's no longer the right fit but failing him and the company because you don't have the courage to do the kind thing. Kindness calls you to tell him he's not the person for the position and then dignify him in the transition."[12] Kindness calls us to be honest in a way that is loving, even if it isn't always nice.

False Joy

Much like kindness, joy is a fruit Christians know they are "supposed" to have. For some of us, this pressure is about our personal image—the desire to look like a particular kind of good Christian—but for others of us, it's about more than that. We want to reflect well on Jesus. We want to convince people to find life in Christ by wearing an ever-cheerful face. And so we turn joy into a work. We paint on niceness in place of true joy, thinking it will get the job done.

The trouble with this false joy is twofold. The first issue is that it's flimsy. In Matthew 7:24–27, Jesus told a parable of two builders, one who built his house on rock and the other who built his house on sand. Jesus didn't mention anything about their appearances or the quality of shelter they provided, but we can assume it was largely the same. Two similar houses that got the job done. That is, until a storm blew in. The wind swirled and the rain beat down and the house on the rock stood firm, but the house built on sand did not. In fact, Jesus didn't simply say the house fell, but that it fell "with a great crash" (Matt. 7:27 NIV).

An exterior of joy is a lot like those houses. False joy can look nearly identical to true joy, and it can maintain the appearance for awhile. The thing that unmasks our joy and reveals its true quality is the hammering power of a storm. Like a hurricane ripping off loose shingles and boards, storms have a stripping quality to them. Financial uncertainty exposes the ways our joy is dependent on our income. Physical setbacks expose the ways our joy is dependent on our health. Aging—which is less of a storm and more of a slow, steady erosion—exposes how much of our joy is dependent on our beauty or our youth. Although God gives us this world to enjoy, storms expose exactly what our joy is standing on.

Another difference between the true fruit of joy and the false fruit of joy is how they arrived on the tree. It's the difference between an apple and a plastic Christmas ornament: one grows directly from the vine while the other does not. One is a product of the tree, the other added later. One is alive, the other is dead.

Galatians 5:22 tells us joy is a "fruit of the Spirit," meaning joy is not a thing we produce. It does not originate with us or our abilities, but instead, it begins with God. False joy, on the other hand, is a performance. It's something we muster up with our own willpower and still, it is never as durable or compelling as the joy that blooms from the Spirit of God.

In addition to being flimsy, false joy is also unconvincing. The world sees through it. People don't trust it. In our effort to convince people of the goodness of Jesus, we end up accomplishing the opposite. We come across as frauds, because the average person knows there is no such thing as infinite cheerfulness. Even Jesus wept (John 11:35), reminding us that unquenchable positivity is not what we are called to, nor does it reflect the human experience.

False joy never lets us rest, and at the same time, it accomplishes little. True joy is the opposite. True joy is attractive and influential, not because of our stiff upper lip but because the fruit of the Spirit can flourish in any climate, sunshine or rain.

False Belonging

Another reason niceness often deteriorates into falseness is that niceness is primarily oriented toward ourselves. We are nice because we want to be accepted, included, and brought in. Sommers puts her finger on this phenomenon.

> Niceness is behaving or talking in ways designed to make us compatible with people and situations. Often when we feel insecure we shore ourselves up by silencing the behaviours and words that we believe might make us less acceptable to others. Silencing may seem innocent enough, but in reality it often means that we compromise ourselves, that we are not honest with our thoughts and feelings.[13]

Sommers highlights silence as an "essential characteristic of being nice."[14] She describes the ways in which we hide our true selves for the sake of relationship.

We believe that being nice will:
- ease the beginning of relationships,
- endear us to people,
- hold relationships together,
- prevent emotional pain for ourselves and others,
- cover up our flaws or unkind thoughts,
- mask our true motives,
- spare us from having to say things that are hard to say, and
- provide us with a peaceful existence.[15]

This is what we count on niceness to achieve, but the sad irony is that this kind of "belonging" only alienates us further. The silencing and hiding of being "nice" means we are pleasant and acceptable but not truly known. Deep down, we know that our acceptance is conditional. In this way, niceness promises something it cannot give. To paraphrase Sommers, we are nice because we fear aloneness, but our niceness only perpetuates it.[16]

A Crisis of Credibility

Very often we turn to niceness because we want to be kind or we want to appear joyful or we want to belong, but niceness misses the mark on all counts. However, there is one more reason we should be concerned about the inauthenticity of niceness, and that is what it does to our credibility as followers of Jesus. When we confuse Christlikeness with niceness, and when we cover up our true feelings and our true flaws in order to present some image that we think will serve the cause of Christ, we are cutting our legs out from under us. As I already mentioned in the discussion of false joy, the world can tell when we're faking it, and they have no interest in skin-deep happiness or superficial love.

Perhaps the biggest lie of all is that Christ's reputation depends on *our* reputations and that people will only be convinced of the gospel if we shine it up with our relentlessly sparkling lives. This deception is oppressive to us, because it burdens us with the pressure to look happy all the time. It is also oppressive to others. This lie is the reason many nice Christian men, women, pastors, and leaders deceive and destroy in order to protect their images. It's the reason whistleblowers are often criticized for hurting a preacher's ministry, instead of being lauded for their honesty and courage. This is all done in the name of Jesus's reputation, as if it is so fragile that it can be shattered by one of the very sinners he came to save.

I hope you know it is not. Jesus doesn't need us to be nice. He doesn't need us to pretend the ugly parts of ourselves are not there. He doesn't *need* anything from us.

Instead, Jesus promises that if we can ditch our nice tendencies and be honest about our brokenness, our hopes, our dreams, and all the ways we need him, there is life to be had—even life to the full (see John 10:10). Author Megan Hill once wrote, "Being authentic means that God and his Word define what is real."[17] If this is what we pursue, not our image and our truth but God's image and God's truth, then that truth will set us free, and we will be free indeed (see John 8:36).

~~~~~~~~ TAKING ROOT ~~~~~~~~

Be on your guard against the yeast of the Pharisees, which is hypocrisy. There is nothing concealed that will not be disclosed, or hidden that will not be made known. (Luke 12:1–2 NIV)

~~~~~~~~ DIGGING DEEPER ~~~~~~~~

1. In what ways is authenticity important to you?
2. How does the inauthenticity of social media affect you?

3. How would you describe the difference between niceness and kindness?

4. Do you ever feel pressure to put on an appearance of joy? And if so, in what circumstances?

5. Have you ever struggled to be authentic and honest with God? If so, how?

3

Rotten

THE FRUIT OF CORRUPTION

"I loved Doug. He was very sweet and kind and nice."

These were the shocked words of an acquaintance who discovered her friend, Douglas Cone, was not the man he appeared to be. Nicknamed "Diesel" for "his penchant for puffing endless unfiltered Kools,"[1] Cone was a millionaire construction magnate who lived in Tampa, Florida. With the exception of his wealth, Cone seemed like a regular "rough and tough" guy with an upstanding family to boot. Married for fifty years, Cone and his wife were noted philanthropists in the community. Their three children had attended a prestigious prep school where the library was named in his wife's honor.[2]

Everything changed in 2003 when Cone's wife, Jean Ann, died in a strange accident. At the age of seventy-five, Jean Ann "was found slumped behind the wheel of her Rolls, its ignition on, in the family's closed garage."[3] Police reports determined she had a blood alcohol level more than twice the legal limit, and her death was ruled an accident. Most likely, she fell asleep after pulling into the garage and never shut off the engine.

Jean Ann's death was shocking because it was sudden, but what stunned Tampa society even more was Douglas's hasty remarriage to Hillary Carlson, just two weeks after Jean Ann's death. Soon the community would learn that Carlson was no spontaneous rebound but the woman with whom Cone had been carrying on a secret life. For years Cone had assumed the alias of Don Carlson and fathered a family just twenty miles away from his home with Jean Ann. Even more shocking was just how much the two women shared in common. Their children were enrolled in the same prep school. Both women had school facilities named in their honor. Both drove Rolls-Royces. And most surprising of all, both served on the school's board of trustees.[4]

It is unclear how much either woman knew about the other, but Cone seems to have maintained the lie by telling each wife he was frequently away on business. Regardless of what they knew, the surrounding community was flabbergasted by his deception. "I had no reason to suspect anything," one female friend lamented. "I still am a little in shock about what happened because I can't believe he would do that to her."[5] She also added, "He seemed so nice."

We have all heard stories like these, of parents, spouses, coworkers, and communities fooled by people they thought they knew, people who seemed so nice and put together on the outside but were hiding something rotten within. This is the second fruit of niceness that I want to explore because it highlights the way that niceness functions like a "social lubricant." It wins us acceptance and praise while providing cover for our vice. Niceness is, in a sense, a safe haven for our sins. It is a refuge keeping our dark secrets hidden from the light. In addition to that, niceness also blinds us to the corruption of others. When we measure, trust, and elevate others based on how nice they are—as opposed to some other, more reliable measure of character—we contribute to a culture ripe for dysfunction and deceit.

As we have already examined, niceness is a false virtue in our culture, which means many of us rely on it to assess another person's character. The trouble is—as Douglas Cone's story demonstrates—niceness doesn't tell us much at all. The nightly news is full of stories of deception, of loved ones blindsided by the secret sins of a seemingly nice person. An abuser. An adulterer. A serial murderer. Somehow these individuals are able to fool virtually everyone they know. Nobody sees it coming, but it's also possible they were looking at the wrong thing.

Blinded by the Nice

Almost every night of the week, my parents have a bedtime ritual that involves true crime television shows. They dim the lights, snuggle up next to one another on the couch, and scan the channels for an episode of *Dateline*. I have never really watched it before, but I know the story lines usually follow a common arc. Somebody dies in a suspicious manner, and it is probably the boyfriend/girlfriend or husband/wife. Clearly the perfect show for a married couple winding down for bed.

A few months ago, I was visiting my parents and decided to join them in the living room. We watched the story of a woman named Christy who met and married her Prince Charming, a man who was thoughtful, devoted, and an all-around nice guy. He was everything she was looking for in a husband.

But this all changed almost immediately after the wedding. It was as if something inside him had flipped. Gone was the loving, gentle man with whom Christy had fallen in love. In his place, a mean, abusive philanderer appeared. Christy was astonished. How had he managed to fool her? How was he able to hide who he really was?

The truth was he hadn't hidden his true self. All along, his character was in plain sight. Years before the couple married, the husband had been married to a close friend of hers. Throughout that first marriage, the friend confided in Christy about the reality of their relationship, that he was abusive and unfaithful. Christy listened to her friend supportively and sympathetically until the marriage eventually fell apart.

Some time after her friend's divorce, Christy became romantically involved with the man herself. Perhaps she thought she could change him or perhaps she thought he had already changed. But for some reason, she expected an outcome quite unlike her friend's marriage. In spite of knowing every sordid detail of that nightmare relationship, Christy married her "Prince Charming" and expected to live happily ever after.

As I watched her bewilderment at her husband's actions, I oscillated between judgment and compassion, between yelling at the TV and wanting to give Christy a hug. She said she was blindsided, but that wasn't really the case. For years, and with her very own eyes, she had seen what this man was capable of. The only "blindness" was self-imposed.

It's easy to watch shows like that and pat ourselves on the back for being wiser than the people on screen, but the truth is, we all do this in some form or another. We give preference to niceness. As my friend Lisa Whittle once told me, if someone treats us well or says what we want to hear, we are "willing to overlook more important things." Niceness makes it all the more likely we will forgive misbehavior—or deny it altogether.

In September 2016, former gymnast Rachael Denhollander became the first of 156 women to publicly accuse Dr. Larry Nassar of sexual abuse. Following her courtroom statement, the judge in the trial commended Denhollander for her courage: "You started the tidal wave. You made all of this happen. You made all of these voices matter."[6]

Unfortunately many of the victims who spoke out against Nassar before Denhollander's breakthrough were silenced. They were pushed to the side or swept under the rug. For decades, young women were subjected to Nassar's abuse. Even when they sought help, their stories were not believed. One article documents eight different cases of women who reported Nassar to an adult or administrator to no effect.[7] In 1997, a sixteen-year-old gymnast turned to her coach for help. The coach was friends with Nassar, so she explained that the girl must have simply misunderstood his treatment methods. In 1999, a runner contacted her coach with a similar complaint but was told Nassar "was a respected doctor and she should trust him."[8] And in 2004, a twelve-year-old friend of the family confided in a psychologist that Nassar had been molesting her since she was six. In this especially heartbreaking story, her parents chose to believe Nassar instead of their daughter. This decision forever fractured their relationship with her, and it may have been a catalyst for her father's eventual suicide.[9]

Case after case reveals multiple layers of systemic dysfunction, including deliberate, institutional self-protection. However, there was an additional layer of brokenness that seemed less intentional, but its consequences were just as devastating. Coaches, colleagues, and neighbors who had nothing to gain by silencing the victims were nevertheless blinded by Nassar's niceness. Nassar's reputation as an upstanding, world-renowned doctor and a trustworthy family friend all carried more weight in their minds, so that is what they saw.

In all of these instances—the woman on *Dateline* and the coaches and parents who ignored Nassar's victims—the truth was hiding in plain sight. The abusive husband had already revealed his true character. The victims had already reported the crime. But people refused to believe it. Instead they put their faith in nice.

Desperate for Discernment

I am not sharing these stories in order to blame people who were fooled, because some deceivers are absolute masters at what they do. They delude everyone they know, even the people who know them best. I am sharing these stories because they testify to the power of niceness to blind us to the truth. Even good people, who know the difference between right and wrong, can miss the evil happening right under their noses. This reality has dire consequences, not just for ourselves but for people we are called to protect.

As I already mentioned, the original context of Matthew 7 is false teaching, and earlier in his warning about bad fruit, Jesus warns, "Beware of false prophets, **who come to you in sheep's clothing but inwardly are ravenous wolves**" (v. 15). Ephesians 5:11 says something similar: "Take no part in the unfruitful works of darkness, **but instead expose them.**" Both of these verses underscore why any of this matters. The problem with accepting the mask of niceness is not that it makes us look silly or reveals us to be bad judges of character. The problem is that when we give inordinate weight to niceness and allow it to cloud our judgment, we open the door to a ravenous darkness. This darkness—this *wolf*—not only intends to devour us but the most vulnerable among us: children, widows, the elderly, the sick, the poor. Wolves prey upon these vulnerable groups by approaching them as lily white sheep. It's the nice young man who calls my grandmother and promises her financial security for "only one thousand dollars down." It's the nice preacher on television who guarantees prosperity to families if they will simply mail him a check. These individuals look nice while in reality they devour, and as followers of Jesus reflecting the heart of God, our relationship to them is not neutral.

The God who is fierce about children (Luke 17:2), widows and orphans (James 1:27), the stranger and the poor (Heb. 13:2; Isa. 25:4; Prov. 14:31, 19:17, 28:27; Matt. 19:21; 1 John 3:17–18), this God calls us to be fierce along with him, and that calling has practical implications for our lives.

In Matthew 10:16, Jesus clarifies just what it means to live as discerning people in the world, saying, "I am sending you out like sheep among wolves. Therefore be as shrewd as snakes and as innocent as doves" (Matt. 10:16 NIV). The word *shrewd* means "having or showing sharp powers of judgment."[10] This definition—along with Jesus's use of the word *shrewd*—reminds us that we can know something is wrong but still be blind to it. We need more than a sense of right and wrong in order to oppose corruption in the world. What we also need is discernment.

Discernment is not something we are born with; it is something we acquire. Scripture offers three helpful guidelines for becoming more discerning, but first I want to clarify what discernment is not.

Discernment can easily flip into paranoia, legalism, cynicism, or a quickness to judge, and that is not what I am advocating here. First Corinthians 13:7 says, "Love . . . hopes all things," which means the command to love others is a command to be hopeful for others. We can be shrewd as snakes, but at the same time hopeful in God's ability to redeem. We ought to hold that tension as tightly as possible.

With that in mind, let's look at three biblical filters that help us discern the rotten fruit from the good.

Consider a Person's Character

If ever there was a book of the Bible packed with guidance for discernment, it's the book of Proverbs. It is filled with wisdom and practical advice for daily living. Throughout the book, it gives instructions for walking the path of righteousness and life versus walking the path of death. Proverbs also provides insight into those who are foolish and those who are wise. In a sense, Proverbs is a primer on character. It draws a sharp distinction between wisdom and folly and corruption and character by depicting very obvious markers of both:

Do not reprove a scoffer, or he will hate you; reprove a wise man, and he will love you. (9:8)

The wise lay up knowledge, but the mouth of a fool brings ruin near. (10:14)

The way of a fool is right in his own eyes, but a wise man listens to advice. (12:15)

There is one whose rash words are like sword thrusts, but the tongue of the wise brings healing. (12:18)

One who is wise is cautious and turns away from evil, but a fool is reckless and careless. (14:16)

The tongue of the wise commends knowledge, but the mouths of fools pour out folly. (15:2)

A fool gives full vent to his spirit, but a wise man quietly holds it back. (29:11)

Humility. Discretion. Gentleness. Healing. These are the marks of wisdom and righteousness displayed consistently, sacrificially, and over a long period of time.

Destruction. Anger. Recklessness. Pride. An inability to listen, to be taught, or to admit wrongdoing. These are the markers of wickedness and foolishness, but niceness can dress them up attractively. Niceness can cloak these warning signals in charisma, flattery, affinity, and false intimacy. Niceness can even hide these traits behind an image of lowliness and humility, and it can do so very convincingly. But it can't do it for long. Eventually its true colors show through, **and we have to be willing to acknowledge when it does.**

That last step is important but tough. When a nice person reveals their corruption—a person we love, a person who loves us, a person who has helped us or even changed our lives—it's confusing, disorienting, and disillusioning. Not only does it come as a surprise but we don't want to believe it's true. That's why it is so important to trust Scripture more than our own intuition.

In Proverbs and throughout the Bible, God is warning us—and helping us—by revealing that character is the greatest predictor of future behavior. The Message version of Matthew 7:15 puts it this way: "Don't be impressed with charisma; look for character." More than what a person preaches on Sunday, professes during Bible study, or proclaims on social media, character will tell you who a person really is and what they truly believe.

This leads us to the second filter for distinguishing between niceness and true character.

Confess Your Bias

James 3:17 says, "The wisdom from above is first pure, then peaceable, gentle, open to reason, full of mercy and good fruits,

impartial and sincere" (emphasis added). Romans 2:11 tells us "God does not show favoritism" (NIV). These verses describe a standard of love and discernment that is free from bias. Niceness, however, has a way of messing with that equation.

As I already shared, Carrie Tirado Bramen writes that niceness is "like having a permanent get-out-of-jail-free card that exempts [people] from acknowledging the consequences of their actions."[11] This is especially true when it is personally beneficial or preferential to let someone off the hook. Sometimes it is just plain convenient to confuse niceness with true character. How many of us have done this in dating relationships? You meet a nice person who treats you well and seems to like you a lot. Occasionally he doesn't respect your boundaries or occasionally she becomes irrationally jealous or he doesn't value faith the way you do, but he is a really nice guy. These rationalizations don't always wind up like Christy from *Dateline*, but it's not difficult to understand how she got there. Sometimes we want what we want, so we see what we want to see.

A similar bias is at work with our friends. We are partial to our friends, but we are especially biased when it comes to those who have supported us through good times and bad. In deeply rooted relationships, we are prone to overlook warning signs and extend the benefit of a doubt because "we know them." This is one way Nassar's abuse was able to continue for so long. While most of us will never find ourselves in such an extreme and tragic scenario, many of us are tempted to downplay character flaws when it is convenient to do so. When it comes to our friends, we are more prone to circle the wagons than earnestly search for the truth.

Finally, this bias influences our judgment when we stand to benefit from it personally. Maybe someone is doing you a favor, giving you an advantage, or providing you with some worthwhile "end," making it convenient to overlook the rottenness underneath.

Bias has a way of skewing reality in our favor. In fact, it permits us to pat ourselves on the back for being discerning, because we so easily discern corruption in *others*. The person selling their soul for influence and advantage. The human rights champion who is suddenly silent about her friend accused of abuse. The church members who cover for their pastor when his integrity has clearly corroded. These instances are easy to see and condemn in other people and other communities.

But when it's you—when it's *your* friend who was there for you when you needed them, *your* pastor who officiated your wedding or preached a message that changed your life, *your* mentor who cared about you and invested in you—that's when the lines get blurry. That's when it's tempting to ignore or downplay corruption and focus on the positive. That's when it's easy to rationalize: "Look at all the good they have done!"

When it is us, in our particular situation, loyalty to a leader, mentor, or friend rarely feels like shameless convenience. It can feel very hard and complex. It can even feel brave. But all too often it is basic partiality, something theologian Dietrich Bonhoeffer called "cheap grace."[12]

Be Quick to Listen

Bias is one reason we engage in harsh judgmentalism, all in the name of discernment. Bias, combined with self-righteousness, produces a campaign thirsty for blood not truth. That's why the final guideline for becoming discerning is not to be hypervigilant about sin but simply to become a better listener. As James told the tribes of Israel, "Let every person be quick to hear, slow to speak, slow to anger" (1:19).

Scripture describes listening as a practice of the wise, especially throughout the book of Proverbs:

A fool takes no pleasure in understanding, but only in expressing his opinion. (18:2)

The way of a fool is right in his own eyes, but a wise man listens to advice. (12:15)

If one gives an answer before he hears, it is his folly and shame. (18:13)

Listen to advice and accept instruction, that you may gain wisdom in the future. (19:20)

When we listen to a variety of voices and counselors, we gain perspective we never would have had on our own, which is why discerning people are careful listeners. Listening is our greatest resource for practicing discernment. Conversely, when people are taken in by niceness, it is often because they refuse to listen to others. It's the young woman who dates a man she knows her family won't like, so she withdraws from them instead of listening. It's the leader who shows favoritism to his buddy without consulting his board because he doesn't want to hear what they have to say.

The term *blind spot* literally refers to the part of the retina that is not able to see, but this term is usually applied to driving. In a car or vehicle, the blind spot is an area of the driver's sight that is obstructed, even with the help of rearview mirrors. The interesting thing about blind spots is that everyone else on the road can see what you cannot. If you try to change lanes and a car is in your blind spot, the driver will likely blare their horn. In that instance, your greatest help is the vision and warning of others.

It's the same in life and faith. There are people and groups who can see our blind spots and they can see them well. They can see corruption we cannot see or corruption we *will* not see. That is one of the many reasons we desperately need to listen. We will find ourselves unable to discern between niceness and true character without the help of a wide and diverse community of people, some of whom we disagree with passionately. This is, however, what it means to be the church. The radical nature of the body of Christ is that we are different, we are many, and we need one another (see 1 Cor. 12). Even when we believe there is nothing we hold in common but Christ, God's design obliges us to ask, "How do I *need* them? What can they see that I cannot?"

This is also why we must resist the temptation to divide from other believers. Throughout the history of the church, the desire for purity, holiness, and correctness has led Christians to separate themselves from one another. Ironically this division accomplishes the opposite, because we cannot prune what we cannot see. And we cannot see our blind spots without the help of people who are standing in a totally different place with a totally different point of view.

From all the stories I have shared in this chapter, I hope it is clear why this matters. Discernment is not just a wise practice. A lot hangs in the balance of our ability to discern niceness from goodness: Justice. Freedom. Rescue. Integrity. Credibility. All these depend on our ability to see what is unseen, to confess our biases, to choose not to be influenced by them, and to humbly listen to those who see our blind spots best.

I pray that we would yearn for a character that is deeper and richer and more life-giving than the superficial appearance of niceness. I pray we would have discernment about our leaders' vulnerability to corruption and humility about our own predisposition to self-deceive. And I pray we can be honest about the places where we fail at this, knowing that, ultimately, we all have a little rottenness inside of us. There is only One who does not, which means we don't have to waste time and energy hiding the worm-eaten places inside of us. We can confess it, and then point to the perfect Savior who heals and redeems it all.

TAKING ROOT

The integrity of the upright guides them, but the crookedness of the treacherous destroys them. (Prov. 11:3)

DIGGING DEEPER

1. Have you ever had the experience of being deceived by a nice appearance? If so, why do you think you missed the signs of corruption?

2. Who are the most discerning people you know and what are some of their main qualities?

3. Do you think it's okay to be partial to your family and friends, showing them more grace than you do others? Why or why not?

4. Who do you think is best able to see your blind spots?

4

Bland

THE FRUIT OF COWARDICE

You might say courage is having a renaissance.

While it has always been a popular virtue, courage has become downright trendy. Books, blogs, Facebook statuses, and Instagram posts abound with exhortations to "Be brave." In 2013, musician Sara Bareilles debuted a wildly popular song called "Brave." It released just a year after Disney produced a movie by the same name. In 2017, over seventy religion and spirituality books were released containing the word *brave* in the title or subtitle. Meanwhile, many Christians claim it as their word of the year, and conferences promote it as their theme.

None of this is necessarily bad, because we need as much courage in the world as we can muster. But all this noise about being brave can drown out the true state of affairs. In reality, our popular notions of courage have become somewhat disconnected from ancient Christian teaching about the topic.

Our language about courage is more often fun and inspiring than it is gritty and sacrificial. *Saturday Night Live* once satirized this empty concept of courage in a parody video set to Bareilles's song. As the singer shouts, "I wanna see you be brave!" the comediennes perform acts of trivial courage, such as declining a party invitation, eating the last cookie, or admitting they have forgotten an acquaintance's name.[1] The video cleverly exposes the shallowness of some of our rhetoric about courage.

Historically the church has had a specific understanding of courage. It is included among virtues like prudence, justice, and temperance, all of which are grounded in the virtue of love. As theologian Thomas Aquinas put it, love "directs the acts of all other virtues,"[2] meaning Christian courage is **enabled by love**— "perfect love casts out fear" (1 John 4:18)—and **motivated by love** (see 1 Cor. 13).

Aquinas's definition gives a very precise focus to courage. For him, Christian courage is not merely about facing your fears but doing so for the express purpose of love. Christian martyrs lay down their lives out of love for God. Martin Luther King Jr. braved persecution because of his love for the oppressed. A mother courageously carries her terminally ill baby as long as possible, all as an act of love.

That is how Christians have traditionally understood courage, as being enabled and motivated by love. However, this traditional notion has been replaced with a watered-down version. Contemporary courage affirms us without necessarily drawing us outward in love. It encourages love of *self*, perhaps, but not necessarily love of God and others.

C. S. Lewis captures this breakdown in his book *The Screwtape Letters*. In it, a senior demon named Screwtape instructs a younger demon in the ways of tempting humans.

> Whenever [Christians] are attending to [God] Himself we are defeated, but there are ways of preventing them from doing so. The simplest is to turn their gaze away from Him towards themselves. Keep them watching their own minds and trying to produce *feelings* there by the action of their own wills . . . When they meant to pray for courage, let them really be trying to feel brave.[3]

Screwtape then adds, "Teach them to estimate the value of each prayer by their success in producing the desired feeling."[4]

Lewis pinpoints the difference between real courage and popular courage, which is that **you can feel brave without actually being brave.** It's feeling brave because a social media influencer declared it to be true. It's feeling brave because you are passionate about a worthy cause—whether or not you have yet stepped in to assist it. It's feeling brave because you just finished reading a book that inspired you. It's feeling brave because you are a woman, a parent, or a friend.

Each one of these scenarios can lead us to courage, but what our culture has done is declare us to be "brave" without context or cause. We just are. Perhaps this is what happens when "brave" becomes a catchall term for self-care, confidence, transparency, recklessness, or simply being a human in the world. All of these things can be brave, but none of them are inherently so.

The rise of fake courage is part of the reason we are experiencing a shortage of the real thing. We are settling for something that sounds good because it affirms the choices we are already making, instead of calling us beyond ourselves. It's a kind of courage that rubs our backs and tells us how wonderful we are, instead of challenging us to die to ourselves. And as a result of all this, it's a courage that tastes bland.

As I reflected on my own failures of courage, I realized that one of the primary reasons I was ill-prepared to exercise true courage when necessary, was that I didn't have any practice. For too long I had settled for nice courage, superficial courage, and inspiring courage, all of which were masking and dressing up the cowardice underneath.

In the second half of this book, we will explore how to "practice" courage—how to strengthen this spiritual muscle in our lives. But for now I want to share a little more about how this false courage became so fashionable and tame, how it manifested in my own life, and how you might be able to identify it too.

Nice Courage

"What if people stop reading my blog?"

This worry loomed over me like an ominous cloud as I stared at my computer, debating whether or not to hit Publish. I was tackling a new topic—a controversial one—and I wondered if people would be angry. I was worried that people would dismiss me forever. Would my "regular audience" hear what I had to say?

Until then I had maintained a relatively safe approach to ministry. My teaching was confined to a short list of topics including God, Jesus, sin, holiness, and spiritual growth. All important subjects, but also relatively cautious ones. When you are a Christian author and speaker, those are the topics you are expected to cover. Even when these topics step on people's toes and push them beyond their comfort zones, they are still viewed as "appropriate."

So that is what I did. For years I stuck to the topics that were expected of me, and I taught them as rigorously as I could. I loved theology and the deep truths of the faith, and I was proud of my teaching. I still am. Looking back, however, I can also spot some holes in my teaching, topics I avoided because they seemed too divisive. "You will lose people," I was warned. "It's not worth it."

I do believe there is some wisdom in this advice. As followers of Jesus, our primary calling is reconciliation, not alienation. We should do what we can to "win" people. Not for our sake but for the glory of God. The only problem is that I wasn't doing it for the glory of God. I was doing it for me. Randy Alcorn wrote, "One consequence of being a people pleaser is failing to say what's true because it's unpopular."[5] That's what I was doing. I was staying safe to protect myself. I didn't want people to be mad at me. I didn't want to receive angry comments or be accused of distracting from the gospel. In short, I didn't want to ruin my image.

This is the tension between "nice" and "brave." When the two intersect, we often have to choose between being brave and being liked. That is why the latest trend of nice courage is so enticing. It doesn't force us to choose. Instead, it allows us to be both. Brave and nice.

For a long time, I walked that line. I justified my cowardice. I excused myself from saying and doing courageous things with very holy language. Over time, however, I noticed three ways my nice courage was standing in the way of obedience.

Nice Courage Isn't Biblical

The first problem with nice, safe courage is that it isn't biblical. The Old Testament is chock-full of prophets speaking hard truths about controversial subjects. Rather than avoid these topics for fear of "losing the audience," God often instructed the prophets to walk headfirst into tension. In a later chapter, we will look at the story of Ezekiel, a prophet dispatched by God to a people he knew would reject him. But Ezekiel wasn't the only prophet who "lost" people.

Prophets like Micah did not mince words when they declared God's judgment over Samaria and Jerusalem. Micah didn't even warm up the audience with pleasantries or affirmation. Instead he launched right in with the statement "Let the Lord GOD be a witness against you," (1:2) followed by incendiary statements like these.

> Woe to those who devise wickedness
>   and work evil on their beds!
> When the morning dawns, they perform it,
>   because it is in the power of their hand.
> They covet fields and seize them,
>   and houses, and take them away;
> they oppress a man and his house,
>   a man and his inheritance.
> Therefore thus says the LORD:

behold, against this family I am devising disaster,
    from which you cannot remove your necks,
and you shall not walk haughtily,
    for it will be a time of disaster. (Mic. 2:1–3)

These words read a bit like an angry, 2:00 a.m. rant on Facebook, but neither Micah nor Ezekiel were alone in being tasked with delivering a hard message. In Malachi 2, the prophet conveys the following graphic message to the religious leaders of the day: "Because of you I will rebuke your descendants; I will smear on your faces the dung from your festival sacrifices, and you will be carried off with it" (v. 3 NIV). Similarly, in Amos 2, God asks his servant to condemn Israel with a long list of transgressions.

This is what the LORD says:
"For three sins of Israel,
    even for four, I will not relent.
They sell the innocent for silver,
    and the needy for a pair of sandals.
They trample on the heads of the poor
    as on the dust of the ground
    and deny justice to the oppressed." (vv. 6–7 NIV)

We are not given any impression that the prophets were sensationalizing God's message, making it angrier or more extreme than God intended. Instead, these men spoke plainly, boldly, and obediently, and this is the biblical precedent we inherit.

To be clear, that does not mean anything goes. Romans 2:4 adds a reminder to the witness of the prophets that it is God's kindness that leads us to repentance. God initiates with grace, patience, and love, and we are called to do the same. But these virtues are not to be confused with niceness, and if niceness becomes our compass, we will find ourselves unable to follow a Savior who overturned tables and rebuked the Pharisees with woes. If no one is ever offended or made uncomfortable by our words, then our lives do not reflect the full spectrum of Jesus's life, or his Word.

Nice Courage Is Self-Serving

The second problem with avoiding controversial subjects is, as I mentioned earlier, that it is not motivated by a love for God and others. Unfortunately our human nature is ever so adept at masking this truth. We ignore our slavery to niceness by rebranding our cowardice as wisdom, stewardship, or even love. I know this temptation well. Both in my teaching and in my relationships, there are some topics I would rather not discuss—true things, important things, *biblical* things—because I don't want to deal with the fallout. I say that I am choosing unity over division, but really, I am choosing myself.

In contrast with a self-serving approach to courage, the Bible's notions of it are always oriented toward God and others. Whether God is commanding Joshua to be "strong and courageous" as he goes into battle (Josh. 1:9), David telling Solomon to be "strong and courageous" as he does the work of the Lord (1 Chron. 28:20), or Paul telling the Corinthians to have courage and stand firm in the faith (1 Cor. 16:13), the focus is always bigger than self.

Does this mean there is never a time to act courageously on your own behalf? Certainly not. The woman who works up the courage to escape from her abusive husband is incredibly brave. Instead, I would define "self-serving" as being *primarily* motivated by comfort, more than motivated by love for God and others. It's motivated by preserving your image, your reputation, your ease, and your power. It is motivated by the idol of self.

Nice Courage Cedes Territory to the Enemy

This one takes a little more explaining, and in order to do that, I want to return to the chapter of Micah I mentioned earlier. In it, God rebukes the false prophets of Micah's day with a relevant accusation.

> "Do not preach"—thus they preach—
> "one should not preach of such things." (2:6)

For a little context, the false prophets were telling Micah "do not preach." They didn't want to hear his message because he was preaching hard and judgmental things. In his commentary on Micah, Old Testament scholar Bruce Waltke explains the situation this way: "The 'pseudo-prophets' represent the political-religious establishment. The self-appointed theologians defending the entrenched leaders would have included priests . . . false prophets . . . and counselors"[6] who refused to prophesy judgment themselves. In other words, the false prophets were protecting their own leaders by refusing to preach the truth about them.

"Micah makes clear that **false prophets not only oppose true ones but try to silence them,**"[7] and thousands of years later, this silencing is still happening, though in a slightly different form. These days, we wrap red tape around topics that are either "too personal" or "too controversial." Both inside and outside the church, we live in a culture whose favorite refrain is "Do not preach to me," either because "it's none of your business" or because "it is a distracting, hot button issue." And so topics like racism, sexism, sexuality, immigration, morality, and family get quarantined as "off-limits." If you want to be liked and you want to be nice, polite company, you will not address these things.

The story of Micah reminds us that this silencing is not new, and one of the main reasons it is a mark of a false prophet is that it puts scriptural truth behind that same red tape. This is what I mean by "ceding territory to the enemy." I cannot imagine a better trick of the devil than to reframe biblical truth as a "private" or "hot button" issue. In doing so, the enemy can silence us on topics that Jesus himself was not silent about.

This is something we cannot allow to happen. We cannot cede this territory. We cannot allow the enemy to determine what we can or cannot say using broken, worldly fault lines. That is not to say we should overcorrect by venting our anger online, descending into name-calling, or condemning people with different convictions than our own, but it does mean that we should teach and promote and follow the *full counsel of God*. It may come with a cost, including pushback and condemnation from fellow Christians, but we must be resolute. We cannot allow cultural controversy to confine Jesus's priorities. If Scripture talks about it, we talk about it. Period.

The Cost of Niceness

Again and again, the desire to be nice and maintain the status quo conflicts with the call to courage. Perhaps you have a friend who is making destructive personal decisions, so you are forced to choose between speaking truth or keeping the relationship. Perhaps you feel called to ministry but your family opposes it, so you are forced to choose between following God or listening to your parents. These are the moments that confront us with our true allegiance. Are we slaves to niceness or are we servants of the one true God? Is our need to be liked conflicting with our call to obey? For many of us, I think that it is.

I want to end this chapter by discussing what's at stake, because it is significant. The difference between true courage and nice courage is not nit-picking. When bravery is sacrificed on the altar of niceness, we lose two things.

Loss of Prophetic Witness

First, we lose our prophetic witness. The term *prophetic witness* might be new to you, because many of us equate *prophecy* with predicting the future. For years I thought prophecy was the ability to foresee events or speak new, inspired truths. I pictured men like Daniel, Ezekiel, and Elijah who figured at the center of dramatic stories and served as mouthpieces for God.

In many ways, those men are perfect examples of prophecy, but not because they called fire down from heaven or slept in lions' dens. What makes them significant is the broader role they played among the people of God.

Prophets in the Old Testament were disrupters.[8] They challenged the status quo. They pruned away the false teachings that had grown up around the truths of God like kudzu on a tree. They spotlighted hypocrisy and exposed the ways in which Israel had become too much like the world, condemning sins like idolatry (Hosea), greed (Jeremiah), and neglect of the poor (Isaiah and Amos).

The prophets' disruptive role meant they were not always well liked. In 1 Kings 19, King Ahab "killed all the prophets with the sword" (v. 1). Others, like Samuel, were honored and esteemed but not because they spoke easy truths and affirming messages. When push came to shove, prophets had to choose between being likable and being faithful.[9]

All of this is important for understanding the term *prophetic witness*. It is the kind of Christian witness that carries on the work of the prophets. If we want to live, lead, and teach in a way that is actually "biblical," then our lives should reflect this part of Scripture. That is not to say we shouldn't talk about the "easier" topics in Scripture, like eternal hope or unconditional love, but we are also called to disrupt the false interpretations and moral blind spots within our community and our faith.

If we fail to do this, if we fail to maintain a prophetic witness in the world, then we will not only fail to be consistently biblical in our lives and speech but we will fail to be set apart from the world. That is the pitfall of a Christianity bound by niceness— one whose highest ideals are to be positive and inspiring. It cannot call us to the courage demanded by biblical prophetic witness. We might be well liked, but we will cease to be salt and light. Our saltiness will lose its taste. We will become bland.

This is also one of the challenges facing Christian leaders today. The pressure to be nice and to maintain as broad an audience as possible competes with the calling to be prophetic. I feel this pressure often, but women leaders like myself are not the only ones facing this struggle. For every article about making money with your blog or having a better marriage, we need leaders who are leveraging their authority to call people to rugged faithfulness. We need teachers who are targeting the idols of people-pleasing and politics and worldly success and helping us to be the actual people of God. And we need pastors engaged in the kind of spiritual formation that resists cultural influence and prepares believers for loving self-sacrifice.[10]

Failure of Courage

This leads us to the second cost of niceness. When we are slaves to popularity, we fail to perform true acts of courage. In his book *No More Christian Nice Guy*, author Paul Coughlin pinpoints this dark underbelly of niceness (emphasis added).

> Now here is where part of the real rub begins. **Nice people actually oppose good people who rock the boat, even when headed toward God's will.** . . . . It was nice and pleasant people who killed the prophets of old, who handed Jews over to Nazis, who opposed Martin Luther King Jr.'s efforts to end segregation. And it was seemingly nice people who yelled to Pilate to release the notorious prisoner Barabbas and crucify Jesus instead.[11]

With these words, Coughlin uncovers the scandal of niceness. When we look at the greatest atrocities in human history, all that evil required was a small group of people to accomplish their wicked goals, while the majority of nice people simply looked the other way. This sort of silent complicity allows nice people to insist on their own innocence, while evil transpires in their midst. It also allows nice people to oppose injustice in theory, while never actually lifting a finger to stop it. And finally, it allows our society—and our churches—to openly reject hate, while quietly nurturing a generation of nice people who passively stand by.

This was the very group of people Martin Luther King Jr. addressed in his "Letter from Birmingham Jail." The letter was directed at eight white clergymen who disagreed with King's marches and penned a statement titled "A Call for Unity." The statement was published in the local newspaper, and King responded with these words:

> I must make two honest confessions to you, my Christian and Jewish brothers. First, I must confess that over the last few years I have been gravely disappointed with the white moderate. I have almost reached the regrettable conclusion that the Negro's great stumbling block in the stride toward freedom is not the White Citizens Councillor or the Ku Klux Klanner but the white moderate who is more devoted to order than to justice; who prefers a negative peace which is the absence of tension to a positive peace which is the presence of justice . . . Shallow understanding from people of good will is more frustrating than absolute misunderstanding from people of ill will. Lukewarm acceptance is much more bewildering than outright rejection.[12]

What is most convicting about this letter is that it was addressed to people who opposed racism. They knew racism was wrong. They said it was wrong. They were nice, decent people. And yet, in the words of King, they became just as great a stumbling block to the freedom of African Americans as those who actively oppressed them. How? Because they were more committed to the status quo than they were to justice. They were more committed to comfort than they were to courage. They had good intentions—great intentions!—but they weren't willing to count the cost for them.

This is the impotence of niceness. We live in a world desperate for true acts of courage, desperate for people who will follow Jesus's lead in forsaking their comfort and leveraging their privilege to help the hurting. The world is crying out for this kind of bravery, but niceness will not call us to these things. It can't. Inevitably, the idol of being liked or keeping the peace runs headlong up against our fear of man or our need to be accepted or our reluctance to displease the people we most desire to please. That is why niceness and courage cannot coexist for very long. Sooner or later, we have to choose a master.

We cannot settle for feeling brave without being brave. Especially those of us who call ourselves Christians. Following Jesus—*truly* following him—means owning up to the truth that there is a cross at the center of our gospel, and we cannot follow him around it. Jesus's love, courage, and sacrifice were not coincidental aspects of his life. His love produced courage and his courage produced sacrifice, which means we cannot claim to be his people if we are unwilling to follow him in this.

When Jesus said that everyone will know us by our love (John 13:35), he did not mean our niceness. What made Jesus's love Jesus's love was not his chipper attitude or his unwavering cheer. What made his love his love was his sacrifice. And *that* is how people will know our love. That we count the cost. That it's not about us. That we are willing to lay down our safety, security, privilege, and comfort so that others would encounter the love of God. That is what Christian courage is and is about. It may not fit on a mug, but it can actually change the world.

TAKING ROOT

For God gave us a spirit not of fear but of power and love and self-control. (2 Tim. 1:7)

DIGGING DEEPER

1. Why do you think words like *courage* and *brave* are so popular in our culture today?

2. What do you think is the difference between "feeling brave" and "being brave"?

3. What topics are Christians most uncomfortable with and most likely to object "Don't preach to me about that"?

4. What are some specific ways you can "practice" courage in your life?

78

5

Bitter

THE FRUIT OF CYNICISM

One of my all-time favorite Christmas movies is *National Lampoon's Christmas Vacation*. Ike and I practically know it by heart, and watching it has become a holiday tradition we look forward to every year. This year I've already watched it several times. (I am writing these words midway through December when it airs on a nearly constant loop.)

If you have never seen the film, it follows the trials and tribulations of Clark Griswold—played by a fresh-faced, forty-something Chevy Chase—a loving husband and father whose vision of Christmas is a high-voltage Norman Rockwell extravaganza. He wants the biggest tree, the best decorations, and all the nostalgia he can muster, so he sets out to achieve his dream. Unfortunately things don't go according to plan, and as the story progresses, Clark encounters setback after setback: He drives his family out into the wilderness to cut down a tree and wrecks his car along the way. He finds the tree only to discover he has forgotten to bring a saw. Once he erects the tree in his house, he realizes it is too big. Meanwhile, he painstakingly mounts thousands of Christmas lights all over his roof but cannot get them to turn on. And as the icing on the stale fruitcake, his bickering in-laws descend upon his home and complain about every single thing. Despite it all, Clark's optimism persists. He is determined to have a good, old-fashioned family Christmas, no matter the obstacles.

Eventually Clark's cheerfulness reaches a breaking point. His extended family takes over the house. The turkey dries out. The tree burns down. A squirrel commences a reign of terror. And to top it all off, Clark discovers his long-awaited Christmas bonus has been replaced with a membership in a Jelly of the Month club. For Clark, this is the final straw. There is only so much a Pollyanna can take, and he snaps. In a matter of seconds, Clark's demeanor shifts from plucky idealism to cold, hard cynicism.

The Source of Cynicism

The word *cynicism* generally refers to pessimism about or skepticism toward other people. One author describes it as having "a low opinion of other human beings."[1] Cynics assume people are "greedy, materialistic, manipulative and hypocritical,"[2] acting mostly out of self-interest. In that sense, cynicism seems completely unlike niceness, which is why this fruit might come as a surprise. We don't expect the sweetness of niceness to produce something so bitter, but Clark Griswold is a perfect example of how niceness can lead to cynicism.

It can develop in a number of ways: slowly over time through a series of wounds or bad experiences or as the result of a bias toward a specific group. But in the case of Clark Griswold and others like him, cynicism springs from a particular kind of niceness that is cheerful and open. This niceness has an idealistic view of the world, insists on the inherent goodness of people, and is fueled by a "give good to the world, and the world will give it back" mentality. Paul Coughlin calls this the "The Niceness Doctrine," which subconsciously believes: "I will treat everyone really nicely, and in return, everyone is obligated to treat me with kindness and respect as well."[3] When this is our mentality, and it gets shattered, we tend to respond with a thicker-skinned view of the world.

In his book *A Praying Life*, Paul E. Miller traces the progression from idealism to cynicism, explaining, "Cynicism begins, oddly enough, with too much of the wrong kind of faith, with naïve optimism or foolish confidence."[4] Miller points out that this "naïve optimism" was actually the result of a shift in society's thinking, one that saw people trusting less in the goodness of God and more in the goodness of people.

To put this another way, niceness and cynicism are two sides of the same coin. Both have a simplistic view of the world: one that is largely optimistic in its outlook and one that is largely negative. When the first outlook fails, we flip to the other extreme. As Miller puts it, our "optimism rooted in the goodness of people" eventually "collapses when it confronts the dark side of life."[5] This collapse can be initiated by wars or economic crises, but it can also occur in our personal lives. Maybe it was the first time a trusted friend lied to us, the first time our pastor was exposed as a hypocrite, or the first time our neighbors chose fear over love. The experience is almost always devastating. And so, in a desire not to be wounded or tricked again, we harden ourselves. We expect the worst. We self-protect. We become cynical.

I will never forget the year my family encountered its own "collapse." It was just before Christmas of my eighth-grade year, when my family came home from a long night out. Earlier that afternoon we had driven south of Charlotte to a tiny town called McAdenville, which was known for its over-the-top Christmas lights. It was an annual tradition of ours—eating barbecue at a hole-in-the-wall restaurant before taking in the lights—so we filled our bellies with pulled pork and hushpuppies, drove through the display, and then headed back to the city. But our night wasn't over yet. We also had tickets to see the Hornets play, so we hustled over to the Charlotte Coliseum and watched the basketball game before returning home around 10:00 p.m. It was a long, fun night.

That is, until we got home.

As soon as we walked through the door, we could tell something was off. There was a strange, musty smell of gas, the kind left behind by a lawn mower or leaf blower. It was unusual, but I was an oblivious middle schooler, so I bounced upstairs to get ready for bed.

My parents began to investigate.

It didn't take long for them to determine the source of the smell. As soon as they entered their bedroom, it was apparent that we had been robbed. Drawers lay everywhere, the contents dumped onto the floor. My mom's jewelry box had been emptied, along with her engagement ring. As my parents traced the disorder around their bedroom, they were startled to discover a giant hole in the floor of their closet. This was, as it turned out, the reason for the smell. The intruders had crawled under the house and used a gas-powered chainsaw to rip through the floor.

We quickly realized this was an inside job. The burglars knew exactly where to enter—squarely in the middle of my parents' closet, right next to the safe. The robbers must have known the floor plan of our house. We had only been living there six months, so we guessed it was one of the many people who had built the house. It was impossible to determine who was to blame—and we never did find out—but this realization was especially crushing for my mom. She had gotten to know the crew and they had gotten to know her, so the robbery felt personal.

That experience forever shaped my parents' sense of security. From then on, we were never allowed to leave the house without setting the alarm, even for ten minutes. Over twenty years later, my parents still deadbolt the door in their perfectly safe condo development full of harmless retired folks. The experience changed their way of seeing the world and, as a result, their way of living in it.

This is, very often, how cynicism is born. In *Faith Without Illusions*, Andrew Byers explains, "Cynicism often arises from painful disillusionment—when the rug gets violently jerked out from under us, when the wool long pulled over our eyes is yanked off. The moment of the defining injury is often abrupt, having the effect of an explosive collision that tosses us into some pit."[6]

Disillusionment is a common path to cynicism. No one likes to be made to look like a fool, and cynicism is one defense mechanism we use to prevent it from happening again. But here is the thing about disillusionment: it does not have to produce cynicism. The word itself literally refers to loss of an illusion—the debunking of a fantasy, a deception, or a delusion—which isn't negative at all. Not if we prize truth.

When our niceness is rooted in illusion or a false belief about the world, it is ripe for cynicism. Whether it's an illusion about a role model, a parent, a friend, or a church, the realization of their brokenness can have a hardening effect on our hearts. But it doesn't have to. Rather than harden ourselves into a defensive posture in order to keep from getting hurt, we can welcome the truth that painful disillusionment brings and allow the pain to prune us, rather than harden us.

The Spread of Cynicism

I will be the first to admit I struggle with cynicism often. If you met me, I doubt you would consider me a cynical person, but just like the other fruits we have looked at, cynicism is an effective hider. Cynicism not only springs from niceness but it also puts on the façade of niceness, though for a slightly different reason than the other fruits we have discussed. For many cynics, the appearance of niceness is not about getting something; it's who we actually aspire to be. We earnestly want the world to be a better place. We genuinely believe Jesus and his followers can change it. And we have worked hard toward those ends. But somewhere along the line, we were disappointed. Other

Christians let us down or we were shocked by the magnitude of the world's brokenness. The problems were bigger and harder and more complex than we ever imagined, and that was the moment bitterness gained a foothold.

That is my story. I swing between what I know God says about people and my call to love them and what I feel when I read the news, go online, or get cut off in traffic, which is that *everything is horrible* and *people are the worst*. My cynicism comes from frustration, disappointment, or even righteous anger that has calcified in my heart. And so I can wax eloquently about hope and unconditional love because that is who I *want* to be. Deep down, for the glory of God, I want to be that person, but all along, cynicism is seething just beneath the surface.

This is a common internal conflict, which is one of the reasons why Miller refers to cynicism as the "spirit of our age."[7] However, there is an additional factor contributing to this "age," which is that cynicism never remains internal. As much as we try to bury it under positivity, cynicism has a way of seeping out, and when we look at Scripture, that is exactly what we see. The word *cynicism* never appears in the Bible, but the word *bitterness* appears quite often.

> See to it that no one fails to obtain the grace of God; that no "root of bitterness" springs up and causes trouble, and by it many become defiled. (Heb. 12:15)

> The heart knows its own bitterness, and no stranger shares its joy. (Prov. 14:10)

> Do not let any unwholesome talk come out of your mouths, but only what is helpful for building others up according to

their needs, that it may benefit those who listen. . . . Get rid of all bitterness, rage and anger, brawling and slander, along with every form of malice. (Eph. 4:29, 31 NIV)

What each of these verses warns about, and what my own experience testifies, is that cynicism will not be contained. It has a way of making itself known and subsequently infecting others. Parents pass it on to their kids. Teachers pass it on to their students. Pastors pass it on to their church. They baptize their jadedness as "realistic thinking"—even "biblical thinking"—and the cycle goes on and on. In my opinion, one of the saddest consequences of cynicism is when we instill it in younger people. This cynicism comes in all shapes and sizes—from passing our prejudices on to our children to painting a grim picture of marriage and family to young couples. When we do this and call it "wisdom," we are planting a seed of despair in their hearts, instead of the hope of the gospel.

The Sin of Cynicism

Although we live in in a cynical time, I would wager few of us consciously consider ourselves cynics. Few of us own our pessimism. Instead, we reframe our cynicism as "realism." This kind of cynicism manifests in the form of concerned laments about "kids these days," the constant belittling of millennials, sweeping, negative generalizations about Hollywood, conservatives, liberals, politicians, lawyers, journalists, Yankees, Southerners, or that family member who always says the wrong thing. Almost all of us have that group—or several groups—about whom we expect the worst, but we would never call it cynicism.

Instead we call it wisdom, a mark of our commitment to God, or our adherence to Scripture. We're "simply being honest." This is "just how it is," and to say otherwise is to be naïve at best and blind at worst.

That is the logic of cynicism.

Of course, all of this begs the question: What is so bad about cynicism anyway? Or as we are more likely to describe it, what's wrong with *simply being honest*? What's wrong with *just being realistic*?

When we look at God's Word, we can discern three primary reasons why cynicism does not align with the character and ways of God. The first relates directly to that word *honest*.

The Dishonesty of Cynicism

Although cynicism and honesty are very often conflated, in truth, they are at odds with one another. Cynicism glosses over the complexities of people and groups, opting instead for one-dimensional stereotypes. Cynicism lives in the realm of absolutes: "All . . ." "Every . . ." "Always . . ." "Every time. . . ." It makes broad brush declarations like, "*All* celebrities are like this . . ." or "The media is *always* doing that . . ." or "She takes that side *every time*." But these statements are not faithful to reality. These stereotypes do not represent the complexities or diversity of any given group. They instead dwell in the land of shallow half-truths. They're not honest; they're cynical.

One of the reasons we know cynicism is dishonest is that it contradicts Scripture's own depiction of humanity. The Bible's portrait of human nature is incredibly layered, defying simple categories like "good people" or "bad people." It includes men like David, who was both a murderous adulterer and a "man after [God's] own heart" (1 Sam. 13:14). There was also Abraham, who "believed God, and it was credited to him as righteousness" (Gal. 3:6 NIV) but also gave his wife to Pharaoh in order to save himself (Gen. 12). And Peter, who was Jesus's disciple and a courageous martyr, but also denied Jesus three times.

If we are going to talk about "being realistic," then we need to speak of "reality" as Scripture defines it. And what does the Bible say about people? It says that humans are made in the image of God (see Gen. 1:27), that we are "fearfully and wonderfully made" (Ps. 139:14), and that for those of us who follow Jesus, we are God's "workmanship, created in Christ Jesus for good works" (Eph. 2:10). But Scripture *also* says that we "all have sinned" (Rom. 3:23), that "none is righteous" (Rom. 3:10), and "if we say we have no sin, we deceive ourselves, and the truth is not in us" (1 John 1:8).

In short, none of us are "all good," and none of us are "all bad." So long as we are humans, we will be broken. And so long as we are made in the image of God, we will reflect his goodness. Our language about people needs to hold these truths together, but cynicism throws them out the window, opting only to see the bad. In this way, cynicism is not "honest" or "realistic" at all.

The Despair of Cynicism

The second problem with cynicism is that it leads toward despair rather than hope, which is why those two qualities cannot coexist. Cynicism operates out of a "case closed" mentality, dealing with people solely according to their brokenness, rather than the possibility of their redemption. This is also why cynicism and love struggle to coexist. Love "hopes all things" (1 Cor. 13:7), the way a parent keeps hoping for their child's salvation or the way a spouse keeps hoping for their marriage's restoration. Love sees the possibility of resurrection, and it operates out of that place. But not cynicism. Cynicism can only pretend to be loving. It can masquerade as "tough love" or "truthful love," but its callousness betrays itself. The targets of cynicism know they are not loved. They know they are not "hoped for." And this is where cynicism corrodes the Christian witness. We cannot be known by our love and we cannot preach a compelling message of faith in Christ if we are fundamentally cynical people. The world will be repelled by our despair, no matter how honest or realistic we think we are.

That's why Scripture consistently challenges us to resist despair. Cynicism is marked by helpless resignation or fatalistic pessimism, neither of which befits the people of God. That doesn't mean despair is wrong or sinful, since Jesus himself fought despair in the Garden of Gethsemane. But despair is not our destination, and hopelessness is not our guide. It is not a virtue to view people cynically. We are called instead to hopeful expectancy, remembering that no person is outside the bounds of Christ's redemptive grace.

For this reason, we are not to be known by our cynicism but by our hope. We "have our hope set on the living God" (1 Tim. 4:10), we "rejoice in hope of the glory of God" (Rom. 5:2), we put on the helmet that is our "hope of salvation" (1 Thess. 5:8), and we "hold fast the confession of our hope without wavering, for he who promised is faithful" (Heb. 10:23). The word *hope* appears in the New Testament over seventy times, because it characterizes the people of God. Thanks to the resurrection, we are a people who hope.

The Disobedience of Cynicism

The third and final problem with cynicism is that Jesus himself was never cynical. We will look at this more closely in a later chapter, but suffice it to say that Jesus had every reason to be bitter. Jesus was hurt and betrayed by the people closest to him. He was mocked by the very people he came to save, and crucified by those he came to forgive. He was humiliated and shamed, though he deserved honor and glory, and still his heart never grew hard or bitter. He persevered in love and hope, and he is our standard. We must not give in to cynicism, because we do not follow a cynical God.

As a final note, I suspect Jesus's lack of cynicism is one of the reasons why he "taught as one who had authority, and not as their teachers of the law" (Matt. 7:29 NIV). Throughout the Gospels, the religious authorities consistently assumed the worst in people. They cast judgments and made assumptions, and this posture undermined their authority. That is what cynicism does: it weakens our authority on the subjects that matter most. Not only can people sense the dishonesty in our cynicism but they can also detect its agenda. Cynicism is motivated either by arrogance or self-protection, but it is not motivated by truth. And people see right through this.

C. S. Lewis wrote, "A man whose mind was formed in a period of cynicism and disillusion cannot teach hope or fortitude."[8]

As much as we want to enlist our cynicism to prove how much we know, cynicism accomplishes the opposite. It reveals our wounds, our pride, or our personal axes to grind, but it does not bolster our authority. Take it from the One who amazed people with his words, without a shred of cynicism to show for it.

⋀⋀⋀⋀⋀ TAKING ROOT ⋀⋀⋀⋀⋀

Love bears all things, believes all things, hopes all things. (1 Cor. 13:7)

⋀⋀⋀⋀⋀ DIGGING DEEPER ⋀⋀⋀⋀⋀

1. Talk about a time you experienced disillusionment. How did it shape you?
2. Is there an area of your life that you feel most cynical about? Why do you think that is?
3. How do you think Scripture might gently push back against your particular form of cynicism?
4. Cynicism hides itself behind excuses like "I am simply being honest" or "I am just being realistic." Jesus was the most honest and realistic person who ever lived, so why does this logic sound so unlike him?

6

Hard

THE FRUIT OF SELF-RIGHTEOUSNESS

"Everyone rebels at some point."

One evening I sat with some friends as we reflected on our lives and our faith journeys. I had just finished sharing my own story of being a nice Christian girl when this pointed statement came my way. It was delivered to me as a prophecy of sorts, a prediction about the years ahead. I was, after all, the odd one in that bunch, the one who had lived a straight and narrow life. Being the nice girl that I was, I never had a dramatic testimony or a prodigal phase of wandering and rebellion. I was raised in the church, and faith came easily to me. As a teen I never stayed out past my curfew, never drank, never smoked, never even had a boyfriend. My weekends were mostly spent at home with my family, doing homework and watching *Doctor Quinn, Medicine Woman*. I led a G-rated life, and I was perfectly fine with that.

I maintained my nice girl status all throughout college and into adulthood. I did all this not only because I liked being nice but because I believed what God said about the world. I say that not to trumpet my virtue or teachability—it probably owes more to a lack of curiosity than a lack of vice—but to explain my personality. I am not a "learn the hard way" kind of person. If you tell me the stove is hot, I don't need to touch it. I will believe you. And for me, faith is like that too. If Jesus tells me certain choices will lead to pain, I believe him. If he tells me other choices lead to life, I believe him. I have never needed to "taste the fruit."

That is not to say I am perfect, or even close. Like every other human being, I have made a lot of mistakes along the way. I have hurt people. I have hurt myself. I have done foolish, foolish things. But I rarely did it in a spirit of open rebellion. I wasn't testing God to see if he was good and trustworthy. I wasn't rejecting his Word because it didn't suit my lifestyle. Most of my sins came down to selfishness, pride, or a lack of self-control, not a conscious dismissal of God.

So there I sat, listening to my friends describe their own years of wandering and pushing the boundaries, their journeys quite different from my own. I must have seemed so naïve, so sheltered, so blind to myself. And that is what prompted their words: "Don't you worry, it's coming. Everyone rebels at some point."

If I'm being completely honest, the comment annoyed me. No one likes being patted on the head like a child who "isn't there yet." I also knew myself well enough to know rebellion isn't my style. As I have already explained, niceness was a part of my identity. I was nice because I needed to be liked. I needed to be accepted. I needed to be thought well of. Niceness was my confidence and my security, and that is another reason why I never rebelled—I needed the affirmation too much.

So I balked at their suggestions. And I continued to for weeks. It was only months later that I realized something: most of my life had been a rebellious phase.

Nice Christianity

One of my all-time favorite musicals is *Les Misérables*. Growing up, my parents had season tickets to the Charlotte Performing Arts Center, which is where I first saw the show live. In anticipation of the performance, we listened to the soundtrack every day to familiarize ourselves with the songs. I was still fairly young at the time, and I will never forget my parents scrambling for the "Skip" button whenever "Master of the House" came on in the car. Of course, all the musical's adult themes went straight over my head, but its spiritual themes did too.

As I grew up in my faith, I also grew up in my understanding of the story. The plot centers on a man named Jean Valjean who goes to prison for stealing a loaf of bread. After his release from a nineteen-year sentence, he breaks parole by robbing a bishop, only to be shown remarkable grace. This unexpected mercy overwhelms and transforms Valjean, who responds by turning his life around.

Years later, Valjean has become a whole new man, but he is still a man on the run. He is pursued by a police inspector named Javert, who holds to a rigid notion of justice. Javert is more about the letter of the law than the spirit of it, which is why he remains unmoved by Valjean's transformation.

Javert's character is a foil to Valjean, with the two men symbolizing different responses to grace. In one pivotal scene, Valjean can finally have his freedom by ending Javert's life, but instead, in a show of undeserved mercy that echoes the mercy of the bishop, Valjean spares Javert. You would expect this grace to transform Javert just as it had Valjean, but it does not. To his last breath, Javert lives by the law and dies by the law.

Few stories contrast the redemptive power of grace with the soul-shrinking power of legalism so effectively. *Les Misérables* is not overtly religious, but it depicts two very different understandings of the Christian faith. The character of Javert represents a kind of nice Christianity that is defined by its adherence to the rules. This nice Christianity sometimes manifests itself viciously—such as the legalistic Christians who once burned heretics at the stake—but more often it looks benign.

I would be lying if I said there wasn't a little bit of Javert inside of me. Like Javert, there was a time in my life when God's commands became an end in themselves. I didn't view his teachings as an expression of his character but as fences I shouldn't cross. And when faith becomes mostly about not crossing fences, the "holiest" thing we can do is draw fences around those fences, creating an even larger barrier to protect us from sin. This way, we can make sure to stay as far away as possible from the things we shouldn't say or do.

This is a constant human temptation, as old as sin itself. If God says "Rest on the Sabbath," then we add, "Don't even walk too far!" If God says, "Don't get drunk," then we forbid alcohol altogether. And if God says, "Don't eat of the tree," we interpret him to mean, "Don't even touch it either." When we can pull this off, when we can stick to the biblical rules *and* the fences around them, we look like the very nicest of Christians.

I was that sort of nice. I followed all the rules and did everything I was told, but behind that pristine exterior was a deeply judgmental heart. My niceness was a source of pride and self-righteousness, and it wasn't long before it manifested itself in some distinctly Javert-like ways. In college, I remember lecturing a boyfriend about his family's drinking habits, not because they were consuming in excess and not because I struggled with alcohol myself but because I thought it was wrong. Period. I was a full-on teetotaler who refused to even associate with anyone who drank.

That was the kind of nice I was: unbending, rule-exalting, and hard-hearted toward anyone who strayed outside my carefully drawn lines. I was the Javert kind of nice, the Pharisee kind of nice. I did what Pharisees do: I drew fences around the fences. And sometimes, I drew fences around *those* fences.

But here's the thing about fences—they separate. They separate us from others, but they also separate us from God. The more fences we draw around God's Word, the further we distance ourselves from it *and* from him. That is how the Pharisees—a group of people devoted to God—could master the law and yet fail to recognize God in their midst.

The Nice Christian's Rebellion

What I have come to realize about Javert, about the Pharisees, and about myself, is that our niceness *is* our rebellion. Like Javert, we don't want grace. To put it another way, **we don't want to admit we need grace.** We are too good for that. So what looks like faithfulness on the outside is actually quite the opposite. Our approach to faithfulness pushes us away from God, rather than drawing us nearer to him.

In a sermon on Romans 7, Tim Keller reveals this particular kind of rebellion in the apostle Paul, a rule follower who lived and died by the law and never had a "rebellious phase" either. Paul was the guy tattle-telling on the rebels. But in Romans 7, he saw his life and faith from a new point of view. For the first time, he realized that at the heart of his obedience was rebellion. He explained:

> I found that the very commandment that was intended to bring life actually brought death. For sin, seizing the opportunity afforded by the commandment, deceived me, and through the commandment put me to death. (vv. 10–11 NIV)

This is a dense passage with a lot to unpack, but the long and short of it is that there are two forms of rebellion against God. The first is what we expect rebellion to look like. The second is just the opposite but just as common: rebelling against God's law and rebelling against God's grace.[1]

Paul's struggle was the latter. Rather than rebel against the law, Paul used the law to rebel against God. Deep down he didn't want God's grace. Or at the very least, he didn't think he needed it. As long as he could check off a list of rules, he could still maintain control over his life. The commandment that was meant to draw Paul to God ended up standing between them instead. In other words, his goodness was his rebellion.

In her book *Wise Blood*, Flannery O'Connor describes a character who knows that the best way "to avoid Jesus [is] to avoid sin."[2] For many of us nice Christians, this is our story. I think this is especially common among people raised in the church. It's hard for us to see our sickness, because we look so darn good. But that's one of the telltale signs of this subtle rebellion: how much you love your reputation, how much you love being a "good Christian," and how committed you are to preserving that image.

In Luke 15, Jesus tells a famous parable about a prodigal son. Like *Les Misérables*, this story features two very different men: a rule follower and a rule breaker. The difference is that these two men are brothers. One is a good, obedient son, while the other rebels, squanders his wealth, and breaks his father's heart. One son stays home, the other leaves.

Like *Les Misérables*, these two men have very different responses to mercy. As soon as the prodigal son realizes his folly, he throws himself at the mercy of his father and hopes it is not too late. To his surprise, his father greets him with open arms, smothers him with kisses, and lifts him up in celebration. The son who ran toward mercy is home again.

The other son, the "good son," has a very different response. In verse 28, after the prodigal son returns, Jesus continues, "The older brother became angry and refused to go in" (NIV). In his indignation, the older brother—the rule follower, the good son—chooses not to join the celebration and **puts himself outside his father's house.**

At the center of this story is a stunning reversal; the two brothers effectively switch places. The older son puts himself outside his father's house, just as his brother once did. Amazingly, the good son's self-righteousness has the same result as his brother's rebellion. At some point in the story, both sons put themselves outside their father's house, and both rejected their father, though in totally different ways.

In this parable we witness the two kinds of rebellion Keller describes. We are all familiar with the prodigal son's kind of rebellion, which is easy to spot because its destruction is more apparent. But the second kind of rebellion, against God's mercy and grace, is trickier to identify because it doesn't look like rebellion at all. The nice Christian appears to be close with God because he is doing what God told him to do. He is living how God told him to live. But for too many of us nice, rule-following Christians, our rule following is our rebellion. Following the rules, being good, maintaining our image, it all frees us from actually depending on God. Because *we've got this.*

For nice Christians like myself, the parable of the prodigal son chastens us with the warning that rebellion may take many forms, but its destination is always the same. It quietly siphons off our peace, steals our joy, hardens our hearts, and most surprisingly, cripples our witness. After all, how can we speak convincingly about grace if our knowledge is only hypothetical?

That is my story. My rebellion came differently. I resisted grace because I didn't think I needed it. Not really. Not on a deep down, desperate, honest-to-God level. For most of my life, my need for grace was theological head knowledge and not much more. It wasn't until I realized that my lukewarm feelings about grace were actually rooted in a quiet resistance to it that I saw my niceness in a whole new light.

The Hard Fruit of Self-Righteousness

Around the Miller house, one of our favorite snacks is guacamole. I use the Chipotle restaurant recipe with red onion, jalapenos, cilantro, and lemon juice. It is both delicious and incredibly easy to make, so long as the avocados are ripe.

If the avocados are *not* ripe, that's a different story. Maybe you have experienced this trial yourself, but attempting to mash an unripe avocado is a bit like trying to squash a slippery rock. Not only does it take twice as long but it doesn't taste nearly as good. Similar to peaches and pears, an unripe avocado is bitter and hard.

Thankfully there is a trick to picking just the right avocado. In addition to squeezing it in the palm of your hand, you can also check an avocado's navel. If the navel is firmly attached, then the avocado is not yet ripe, but if the navel comes off easily, the avocado is ready to serve.

When I was trying to determine what bad quality of fruit best describes the self-righteousness of nice Christianity, I chose the word *hard* because of examples like Javert, the Pharisee, the good son, and myself. There is a type of nice Christianity that is unyielding in its application of Scripture, and this hard-and-fast adherence to the rules eventually produces a hardness of heart.

An avocado is hard because it is unripe, and that is also true of self-righteousness. We tend to assume rigid religion is a sign of hyper-faithfulness, but really it's the sign of an underdeveloped faith. Many of us use legalism as a spiritual crutch, preferring neat and tidy categories that don't require us to think, trust, walk in faith, or get any dirt under our nails. While God does call us to practices like self-discipline, holiness, and radical obedience—practices the Pharisees loved!—they were never meant to serve as an escape from the mess and complexity and mystery of living our faith in the world. Instead they were meant to equip us for it.

A hardened faith is not truly interested in engaging the world and seeing it redeemed; it's mostly interested in judging it. Thankfully, like the avocado, there are ways to discern the unripeness of self-righteousness in ourselves.

Your Response to Grace

The first sign of self-righteousness is one we observe in the parable of the prodigal son: **how you respond to the grace shown to others.** How do you respond when that church member who is less committed, or less upright, receives more leadership responsibilities? How do you respond when a coworker who doesn't work as hard gets the promotion you wanted? How do you respond when your parents forgive your sibling for the fiftieth time? Can you embrace the wild and windy beauty of grace or do you begrudge it? Does it direct your gaze toward the undeserved grace you have already been given?

These questions are a great tool for diagnosing your motives and your heart with one big qualification: God's grace should never be deployed as an excuse for injustice, as if oppression reflects the unpredictable favor of God. Nearly every Old Testament prophet forbids us from this kind of silence, so when we excuse corruption or injustice on the basis of "grace," we are usually doing so for convenience's sake. When we enlist "grace" to protect ourselves, our causes, or our people, it is a self-serving cheap grace that has nothing to do with the real thing.

That qualification aside, God constantly topples our notions of fairness. With statements like "God has mercy on whom he wants to have mercy" (Rom. 9:18 NIV), God unmasks any part of ourselves that believes we are earning our place next to him. When this happens, when we feel the pain of our self-righteousness, which flails against the extravagant grace of God, we have a choice to make. We can groan and complain, or we can thank God with every fiber of our being that this undeserved grace is the only reason we have any hope at all.

Your Response to Criticism

The second sign of self-righteousness is a cousin of the first: **how you respond to constructive criticism.** The word *constructive* is an important qualifier here, because not all criticism is valid, informed, helpful, or edifying. That said, the self-righteous person resists even the gentlest, most thoughtful feedback. Self-righteousness wails with indignation, "I was only doing my best!" "I meant well!" "You don't know how hard I have it!" "Why aren't you criticizing those other people who are *worse?*" Self-righteousness distracts, diverts, defends, and shifts blame. Nice Christianity does this, because it is more committed to image than substance, and it resists surrendering the charade. Criticizing the self-righteous nice person is like trying to pin Jell-O to a wall.

Humble and teachable individuals are the opposite. They are able to receive criticism, no matter the source. Famous author Corrie Ten Boom once said: "Our critics are the unpaid guardians of our souls."[3] Even unfair criticism, or criticism delivered badly, can teach you something you need to know. It can have the effect of curbing your pride, which is a pain we should all gladly welcome.

No One Thinks They're a Pharisee

It has been two thousand years since the Pharisees faced off with Jesus, but human nature has not changed a bit. We are still drawing fences around fences, straining out gnats while swallowing whole camels of pride, greed, malice, and envy (see Matt. 23:24). This type of hypocrisy is one of my personal pet peeves, and whenever I encounter it, a part of me wants to sit the person down, look them in the eye, and ask, "Exactly *who* do you think the Pharisees are today, if not *you*?"

However, I have come to recognize a funny irony in that question. That is exactly the kind of question a self-righteous nice person would ask, the kind that distracts from its own sin to focus on the sin of others, the kind that is smug and self-satisfied and quick to condemn. Because here is the convicting truth I am just now starting to realize: my "nice Christianity" is changing.

When I was younger, my nice Christianity looked like rule following. I was a cheerful Pharisee who cared deeply about the law. But these days, my nice Christianity looks totally different. My niceness is less legalistic and more aware of the world. My niceness is educated, informed, and culturally sensitive, none of which is inherently wrong in the same way that rule following is not wrong. What distorts both of these versions of Christianity is their motivations. When these practices are placed in service to upholding a certain image or standing over people to judge them, then it's the problem of nice all over again. My latest version of nice Christianity has a different standard of goodness, but it is just as prone to condemn, just as averse to receiving criticism.

Pride doesn't care what your theology is. It doesn't care what you believe or how nice you are about it. Pride will make its home just about anywhere. The only way to combat this is to follow the lead of the prodigal son—run back to mercy. Confess your desperate need for grace. Again and again, run back to the wide-open arms of the Father. Whether you rebelled against God's law or you rebelled against his grace, the broken human soul is constantly drifting away from its port. So return. Repent. Quit with the charade, admit you are wrong, and receive the good news that it's so much better being loved than being nice.

〰〰〰〰〰 TAKING ROOT 〰〰〰〰〰

For by grace you have been saved through faith. And this is not your own doing; it is the gift of God, not a result of works, so that no one may boast. (Eph. 2:8–9)

⋀⋁⋀⋁⋀ DIGGING DEEPER ⋀⋁⋀⋁⋀

1. Looking back on your life, do you notice any "fences" that you drew around God's Word?

2. Are you more likely to rebel against God's law or against God's grace?

3. How do you respond to constructive criticism? In what specific ways could you receive it better?

4. What does "nice Christianity" look like for you? What is the image you are tempted to put on?

7

Processed

THE FRUIT OF SENTIMENTALITY

When Ike and I first started dating, I discovered something about him I could hardly believe. He was an American kid, born and raised, who had somehow made it into adulthood without ever—not once in his life—going to Disney World.

I realize now that this is not out of the ordinary, but at the time I was absolutely scandalized. I had grown up going to Disney every few years. It was a staple of my childhood and a "magical" one at that. My birthday frequently coincided with spring break, so I have numerous memories of blowing out my candles while a bevy of Disney characters stood nearby. Disney was *a part of me*, and Ike needed to understand it!

So shortly after we got married, we took our first trip to Disney. Ike still teases me about that flight down, how I couldn't contain my excitement and stared out the window with a grin fixed on my face. He looked at me in total bewilderment. At one point he accused, "You are more excited about Disney than you were about our honeymoon!" I didn't deny it. "It's a different kind of excitement!" I explained.

Soon after we arrived, I skipped down Main Street in pure ecstasy. I loved bringing my husband to the site of my favorite childhood memories, a joy that later multiplied when we returned with our kids. There is something almost sublime about inviting the people you love into the cherished moments of your past.

Of course, I am not the only one who feels this way about Disney World, because Disney has mastered the art of manufacturing experiences. From the moment you walk through the gates, every step you take is orchestrated to create a fully immersive experience. Every staff member is smiling, every shrub has a backup, and despite the thousands of people who walk its streets every day, the grounds are immaculate. Everything you see, hear, smell, and taste is painstakingly engineered. Infused into all of it is a calculated nostalgia for ages past.

The Disney experience is effective and alluring because it offers us a world detached from reality. It is a world untouched by the brokenness and discomforts of everyday life, a world where everyone is happy and nice and eager to help you, a world where there is no crime, no injustice, no litter, and almost no discomfort at all. It is an experience of joy divorced from the grit and grime of life on earth. All of this is done for the purpose of achieving a "magical experience." And by "magical experience" they really mean "emotional experience," one that people pay lots of money to visit again and again. In that sense, what Disney is selling is not just happiness but *sentimentality*.

What Is Sentimentality?

Sentimentality can be defined in a number of different ways, but it usually refers to a strong expression of positive emotion. The sentimental person has "unusually strong emotional attachments to events, objects, places, eras and beliefs."[1] This might describe how you feel about a family keepsake, a favorite meal, or a childhood vacation spot, all of which are "sentimental attachments."

Sentimentality is common and normal, but it is not always tethered to what is real. For example, one of the reasons people hoard their belongings or find it so difficult to throw away items they will never use is their sentimental attachment to those things. Sentimentality makes it hard to see our possessions or experiences objectively.

Not only is sentimentality untethered from reality but it views reality through a very specific lens. It focuses on what feels good or looks good, instead of the whole picture. Writer Benjamin Myers put it this way: "Sentimentality is emotional satisfaction without emotional connection."[2] Sentimentality "offers us the dubious chance to feel while bypassing the messiness of any real human engagement: not too much feeling but too thin an experience."[3]

That disconnect—between emotion and reality—is probably the best way to understand sentimentality and why it is inherently superficial. Sentimentality is the glowing eulogy for a person who lived a mostly self-centered life. It's the romanticized depiction of earlier civilizations, overlooking the injustices they committed. Sentimentality has a selective memory that tells a good story, whether or not that story is entirely true.

Sentimentality becomes problematic for Christians when it intersects with our faith. A sentimental faith is warm and fuzzy and very *nice*, because it isn't about Jesus so much as the aspects of Christianity that make us feel good: nostalgic childhood memories, family keepsakes, and uplifting statements. A sentimental faith is inspiring, encouraging, appealing to all, and offensive to none, and there is no better example of this pleasing form of Christianity than the festivities surrounding Christmas.

Although Christmas is a Christian holiday, it is almost universally celebrated throughout Western culture, because Christmas isn't necessarily about Jesus anymore. You can flip on the television and hear any number of declarations about what Christmas "means":

- Christmas is about family.
- Christmas is about giving.
- Christmas is about love.
- Christmas is about being together.
- Christmas is about helping people.
- Christmas is about home.

For many people, Christmas isn't about Jesus so much as it is a vague, happy feeling. Christmas is tied to our memories and our nostalgia, and these feelings are powerful, which is why so many people celebrate the holiday regardless of their beliefs about Christ.

I will be the first to admit I shamelessly feed into this sentimental version of Christmas through my love for Hallmark

Christmas movies. The plotlines are predictable, the characters' chemistry nonexistent, and the stories have nothing to do with Jesus, but I am a total sucker for that combination of romance and holiday cheer! In a world of division and fighting and violence and fear, sentimentality offers a warm and fuzzy escape that I welcome each year. So basically I am part of the problem.

But here's the thing, as worrisome as it is that Christmas is becoming increasingly disconnected from the birth of Jesus, the solution is not as simple as "putting Christ back in Christmas." Why? Because his absence is only a symptom of the broader trend of sentimental faith that is popular today.

Sentimental faith follows a Jesus who is porcelain-skinned and smiling, a man who never says a hard or judgmental word. This faith submerges itself in Christian subculture—music, jewelry, artwork, movies—without ever diving into the deep things of God. This faith honors the traditions of parents and grandparents, whether they are biblically sound or not. This faith offers easy answers to hard and complex questions, because mystery doesn't feel very good. This faith skips over the despair of Good Friday to celebrate the joy of Easter Sunday. And this faith is more prepared to wear a cross than it is to carry one.

These sentimental expressions are not after Jesus but a *feeling*. Sentimental faith makes us feel good in the moment, but the gospel of Jesus doesn't always offer us this. As a result, many of us find a way to have our cake and eat it too. Just like the Israelites in the wilderness who fashioned a golden calf to cater to their desires, we have fashioned a Jesus who offers us an escape from the world instead of following the Jesus who leads us straight into it.

Sugary Faith

Unlike self-righteousness or cynicism, which are the hard and bitter fruits of niceness, sentimentality is different. It looks good on the outside, but it tastes good too. It is sweet and addictive and it goes down incredibly smooth, but it has no substance. It's not like a summer strawberry picked straight off the vine. It's processed.

At this point I am using Jesus's metaphor very loosely because Matthew 7 was, without a doubt, not referring to processed fruit. Even so, I couldn't think of a better way to describe sentimentality. When my sons choose the fruit cup to go with their meal at Wendy's, those tiny peach cubes are *perfect*— perfect color, perfect consistency, perfect taste. My boys could eat them all day, but the amount of sugar inside them nearly cancels out any nutritional value. The fruit is sweet but virtually empty of substance.

This is, in many ways, what our culture has done to Christmas. We've turned it into a sentimental day rather than a holy one. We do it to Easter when we focus on the empty tomb while downplaying the cross. And we do it in our daily lives as well. When the substance of our faith is about family heritage or what inspires us or what makes us *feel good*, we are straying into the realm of sentimentality. These processed feelings allow us to put reality in the back seat while niceness takes the wheel.

This feel-good faith takes many forms, but you can recognize it by its quick and easy responses to difficult situations. One writer cataloged the spiritual catchphrases of sentimentality as follows:

- "Things will work out."
- "The most important thing is your health."
- "They're in a better place."
- "You can do anything you set your mind to."
- "He's a good guy."
- "Follow your heart."
- "All good things must come to an end."[4]

These truisms allow us to dodge the hard and unsearchable parts of life, all of which leave us feeling uncomfortable. Sentimentality focuses on what is positive, encouraging, and nice. The trouble is, when spiritual clichés, upbeat music, inspiring Instagram posts, and motivational wall art become the core of our daily discipleship, we possess a sweet and sugary faith whose fruit appeals to everyone but satisfies no one. On its face, sentimental faith appears stable, but there is little underneath to support it. It's a faith oriented more toward the comforts of Jesus than Jesus himself.

The Dark Side of Sentimentality

All of this might seem fairly harmless, but the reason I am devoting a whole chapter to the processed fruit of sentimentality is because it can easily be hijacked for lesser, and sometimes devilish, ends. Sentimental faith is centered around how we *feel*—as opposed to Christ, who transcends our feelings—and focusing on our emotions makes us easy to manipulate. Advertisers do this by luring customers to buy their products with emotional ad campaigns, and Disney does it masterfully as well. But the truth is we also do it to ourselves.

The Deceptiveness of Feelings

A saying that is often attributed to W. B. Yeats warns, "Rhetoric is fooling others. Sentimentality is fooling yourself."[5] Sentimentality tricks us into believing that a feeling means something, whether or not that is the truth. Nostalgia, for example, deceives us with an overly simplistic view of the past. It's the kind of selective memory that looks back on the fifties as "the good ol' days" when entertainment was wholesome and families were intact. This particular form of nostalgia conveniently ignores the racism and sexism of that era, as well as the secret lives of politicians and movie stars who donned a pristine image on-screen while engaging in salacious lifestyles off camera.

Sentimentality is able to pull off this illusion through the power of emotion: *if it feels real, then it must be real.* That is the lie of sentimentality, and the reason it is so dangerous is that emotion can be manufactured by just about anything. The book that galvanizes you to change the world with faint lip service to Jesus. The transcendent feeling of the mountains or the sea. The song lyrics that bring tears to your eyes. The cleverly written TV show. The well-produced commercial. Some of these things are good and lovely and can even echo the character of God, but the last example—a well-produced commercial—points to how easily our emotions can be manipulated.

That is not to say emotions are bad or even inherently deceptive. God made us emotional creatures, and that means our emotions reflect his image just as much as our own. Our emotions give us perspective that our intellect does not. But if we determine truth based solely—or even mostly—on how something makes us feel, it becomes easy to replace Jesus with something that "feels" like Jesus. This misplaced motivation not only produces in us a shallow faith but allows us to justify very un-Christlike behavior as well.

The Fragility of Feelings

Sentimental faith is emotion-driven. It exists to lift our spirits and make us feel better. It is a little bit like plugging your phone into an outlet to charge the battery. We go to church and hear an exhilarating sermon or participate in passionate worship, and it charges us up. We turn on upbeat Christian music, and it charges us up. We scroll through social media and read inspirational posts, and it charges us up. We hang phrases or verses all over our walls, and reading them charges us up. Sentimental faith has an instant emotional payoff that we can turn to throughout our day.

Most of these practices do have a healthy place in Christ-centered faith. Philippians 4:8 tells us, "Whatever is true, whatever is noble, whatever is right, whatever is pure, whatever is lovely, whatever is admirable—if anything is excellent or praiseworthy—think about such things" (NIV). Whatever focuses your gaze on God, I am all for it!

The dynamic I want to name, however, is the myth that the gospel will make us feel good all the time. Or even that it should. In the Garden of Gethsemane, Jesus agonized so deeply that he wept actual blood, which means following him will not always "feel good." In addition to that, we will likely endure seasons of grief and depression so dark that no positive song can lift us out of it.

This is so important to acknowledge, because sentimental faith is not equipped to walk us through the valley, and when we realize this, it can be disillusioning. It can feel as though our faith has failed, and in some sense, it has. But it was not the gospel that failed; it was an empty, emotion-driven shadow of the gospel that failed.

This is one of the many reasons why author Joni Eareckson Tada has rejected a "sentimental Jesus." In 1967 Tada was an active seventeen-year-old girl who loved swimming, riding horses, and exploring the world around her. She was a regular teenage girl living a regular teenage life, but all that changed the instant she dove into a shallow end of the Chesapeake Bay. On that summer day, she fractured her spine and became paralyzed from the neck down. She spent the following two years processing the reality of her new life.

Over the years Tada has become a well-known vocal advocate for people with disabilities, and she has written over forty books. She has inspired countless people with her message of hope and freedom in Christ, a message that is full of resilient joy but is not the least bit sentimental.

Tada explains this balance in tone.

Here at our ministry, we refuse to present a picture of "gentle Jesus, meek and mild," that tugs at your sentiments or pulls at your heartstrings. That's because we deal with so many people who suffer, and when you're hurting hard, you're neither helped nor inspired by a syrupy picture of the Lord . . . when your heart is being wrung out like a sponge, when you feel like Morton's salt is being poured into your wounded soul, you don't want a thin, pale, emotional Jesus who relates only to lambs and birds and babies.[6]

She goes on to describe why so many people still prefer a sentimental version of Jesus: "A sugar-coated Christ requires nothing from us—neither conviction nor commitment."[7]

Tada is exactly right. Sentimental faith is appealing in the way that cellophane-wrapped snack cakes are appealing. Oatmeal Creme Pies are delicious, but you cannot live on them. Too many sweets, or too much sentimentality, will eventually make you sick. Sentimental faith is handing out Twinkies while the world is starving for a home-cooked meal. As theologian John Piper once put it, "The greatest enemy of hunger for God is not poison but apple pie."[8]

Jesus knew this, so he offered freedom, hope, and joy. But he was not sentimental and his gospel was not nice. Jesus was bold, clear-eyed, and unafraid to engage with the brokenness of the world. His hope was not born out of a self-imposed blindness to the hard things around him. He walked directly into the hard things and resurrected them. That is what makes his message so compelling and enduring; it is rooted in something real. At no point did Jesus need to sugarcoat things in order to preach hope.

A Better Gospel

One of my professors in seminary, theologian Stanley Hauerwas, was fond of saying, "The greatest enemy of Christianity is not atheism, but sentimentality."[9] I will never forget the first time I heard this. At the time it didn't make any sense to me at all, but over the years I have come to understand what he meant.

As an inhabitant of the Bible Belt—a region where the majority of people grow up hearing about Jesus and can find a steeple on nearly every corner—Christianity is the air I breathe. If you were raised in the Bible Belt, you probably grew up in church, and sentimentality is the most common form of religion among people who are mostly Christian in name.

Within this culture, where everyone is a Christian whether they are actually following Jesus or not, we are witnessing a growing group of "Nones"—people who were raised in a particular religion but no longer identify with any group at all.[10] What is noteworthy about this group is that they have heard the gospel. They have heard about Jesus. But they are not compelled by either anymore.

I believe this is one of the consequences of nice Christianity disguised as sentimental faith: an uncompelling message and an uncompelling life. However, the answer is not simply rigor or rightness; the answer is richness. We don't need to simply work harder at sharing the gospel; **we need to share a better gospel**. I don't mean we need to improve upon the message Jesus taught, but we must be truer to its message, its complexity, and its depth. Just consider for a moment what God's Word teaches. In place of sentimental platitudes, we encounter the paradoxical mix of darkness and hope.

Not the false hope of "Things will work out" but "Be joyful in hope, patient in affliction, faithful in prayer." (Rom. 12:12 NIV)

Not the false assurance of "The most important thing is your health" but "So we do not lose heart. Though our outer self is wasting away, our inner self is being renewed day by day." (2 Cor. 4:16)

Not the false comfort of "They're in a better place" but "Jesus wept." (John 11:35)

Not the false promise of "You can do anything you set your mind to" but "My grace is sufficient for you, for my power is made perfect in weakness." (2 Cor. 12:9 NIV)

Not the false character assessment of "He's a good guy" but "There is no one righteous, not even one." (Rom. 3:10 NIV)

Not the false wisdom of "Follow your heart" but "Trust in the LORD with all your heart and lean not on your own understanding." (Prov. 3:5 NIV)

Not the false optimism of "All good things must come to an end" but "Consider it pure joy, my brothers and sisters, whenever you face trials of many kinds, because you know that the testing of your faith produces perseverance." (James 1:2–3 NIV)

Sentimental faith feels good, sounds good, and looks incredibly nice, but it doesn't represent the whole truth so it cannot satisfy the human soul. In contrast, the gospel of Jesus Christ requires a lot, feels uncomfortable, and can even be difficult to understand, but it is the only source of lasting peace, resilient joy, and enduring freedom. It may look ugly—like a terrible, rugged cross—but it's the nourishment we truly crave.

∿∿∿∿∿ TAKING ROOT ∿∿∿∿∿

And this is my prayer: that your love may abound more and more in knowledge and depth of insight. (Phil. 1:9 NIV)

∿∿∿∿∿ DIGGING DEEPER ∿∿∿∿∿

1. Having read this chapter, how would you describe sentimental faith to someone?
2. Where can you identify sentimental faith in yourself or in your church?
3. Feelings can be manipulated, but they are not inherently bad. What is a healthy way to discern the truth of your feelings?
4. Why is sentimental faith ultimately unsatisfying?

8

Cultivating a Better Tree

One summer in my midtwenties, I joined a team of college students on a mission trip to Malaysia. We were there to meet students and connect them to a local ministry, but we also spent some time sightseeing in the area. We scaled the Petronas Towers in Kuala Lumpur, which were once the tallest buildings in the world. From there we drove to the Batu Caves, a giant Hindu shrine known for the 140-foot gold deity posted at the entrance of the site. As we climbed the 272 steps up the side of the mountain, tiny mischievous monkeys tried to snatch our snacks.

It was all larger than life and an adventure I will never forget, but out of all the experiences from that trip, there is one memory that is especially seared into my brain: the smell of the durian fruit.

Native to countries like Indonesia, Malaysia, and Thailand, durian looks like a small, aggressive cantaloupe. It has a pale, mustard interior with a golden-brown rind covered in spikes.

However, what makes this fruit so memorable—or should I say *infamous*—is its smell. One food writer described durian's odor as a combination of "turpentine and onions, garnished with a gym sock."[1] Chef Anthony Bourdain warned that after tasting it "your breath will smell as if you'd been French-kissing your dead grandmother."[2] The smell is so strong that high-end hotels have banned it from their lobbies.

There are some people who love the smell and taste of durian, but I can only assume they are the same type of people who love juice cleanses or giving birth. Riding through the streets of Malaysia with the windows down, I could immediately tell when durian was nearby in the same way you can tell when you are downwind of a garbage truck.

Up close, durian was even worse. The texture of the inside was unlike any fruit I had ever seen. Some people liken it to custard—almost like an overripe avocado—but it's more like the fruit equivalent of liver. When you crack it open, it literally looks like a yellow cow organ nestled inside.

For weeks my Malaysian friends urged me to try it. I knew this was solely for their own entertainment, but eventually I gave in. I thought I might as well experience as much of the culture as I could, right?

I picked up a spoon and dipped into the center, shivers running down my spine. As the fruit touched my lips, all my fears were confirmed. It was ghastly. I gagged. And of course, everyone else laughed.

I am going to offer the lukewarmest of apologies to any dear readers who like durian—obviously God created our taste buds differently!—but this is the kind of fruit I imagine when I read

Jesus's words about bad trees bearing bad fruit. The durian tree helps to illustrate why Jesus's imagery is a powerful metaphor for sin, and it does this in two ways.

First it clarifies that **the fruit is not the problem**. Not really. The fruit is the product, not the cause. The problem is the tree. Just as durian trees produce durian fruit, bad trees produce bad fruit.

In reality Jesus was not referring to a durian tree, or any tree that produces weird fruit. Most likely he was referring to a sick tree, because sick trees produce all sorts of bad fruit. Perhaps the tree in the metaphor was diseased or its roots were damaged or the soil was bad. Regardless, the fruit of the tree reveals the state of the tree. Our faith is the same; the fruit of our faith reveals the health of our souls.

This leads us to the second lesson from Matthew 7, which is that **it's not enough to prune the fruits**. Whenever we identify some brokenness in ourselves—an addiction, an unhealthy habit, a personal vice—our immediate reaction is to *stop*. "I just need to *stop* visiting that website." "I just need to *stop* gossiping with my friends." "I just need to *stop* blowing up at my kids." Or for the purposes of this book: "I just need to *stop* turning to niceness instead of true courage, kindness, and love."

Our first inclination is to cut off the fruit. This is not an unhelpful step, but Matthew 7 also reminds us that this solution is short term. If there is durian growing in our yard and offending the neighbors with its smell, it is not enough to pick the fruit but leave the tree. Over time the bad fruit will grow right back. The only way to rid ourselves of durian entirely is to chop down the durian tree.

Sometimes there is sin in our lives that God wants to uproot and throw into the fire—idols of success, of acceptance, of self. Other times, God simply wants to prune our souls so that we can yield a better fruit. But whatever the cause of the bad fruit, we cannot solve the problem without addressing the tree. Something deeper is needed.

The Biggest Obstacle to Growth

This leads us to the second half of the book—the work of cultivating a better tree. But before we get to that, I have a bit of a confession to make. Although I have used a gardening metaphor all throughout this book, I am using it for one reason and one reason alone: because Jesus uses it. It is not because I know anything at all about plants. I am actually pretty terrible with anything planty. I had to conduct a fair amount of research in order to speak knowledgeably about even the most basic practices of gardening because the fact of the matter is I kill plants.

I am not an *intentional* plant killer, mind you—call it a "brown thumb"—but I do not have the gift of horticulture. Last year for my birthday, a close friend left a potted lily on my doorstep, and I made it my personal mission to keep that flower alive. I placed it on my kitchen windowsill to give it just the right amount of light. I watered it frequently but not too much. I methodically picked the dead leaves off the stem. I did all the right things, and for months—*months!*—the plant survived. New buds emerged and bloomed and the old ones fell away. I thought I had broken the cycle of death. I was successfully keeping a plant alive.

But my triumph was short-lived. As the months went by, each stem eventually withered and died until I pruned the very last one. I hoped this was all part of its natural cycle—life, death, and rebirth—but the writing was on the wall. For this plant, there would be no resurrection.

One of the reasons I don't know how to successfully nurture a plant is that no one ever taught me the steps. I don't know the first thing about gardening, but even if I did, every plant is different. Some plants need more water, some need less. Some plants need lots of natural sunlight, some are easily scorched. In order to tend a plant well, you have to study and learn, but you also have to follow the steps. If you forget to water a plant for too long, fail to prune it or thin its fruits, the plant will suffer and perhaps even die.

This aspect of gardening is important as we pivot toward the second half of the book. Too often our approach to spiritual growth is the equivalent of handing someone a plant—someone who doesn't know the principles of gardening, someone like *me*—and ordering them to "Make it grow!" No matter how loudly and convincingly we demand growth, they will be unable to cultivate the plant because they simply don't know how.

Unfortunately this is often how we talk about spiritual growth. As I was preparing to write this book, I read an article about the fruit of the Spirit in which the author concluded that all we have to do is abide in Christ. That was the end. And you know what? The author was exactly right—we *do* need to abide in Christ—but the problem is that many of us don't know *how*. It's our greatest obstacle to spiritual growth; we don't know what steps to take. We want to grow, we want to cultivate something new, but the only direction we have been given is "Grow!"

I want to provide you with habits of growth to replace the habits of niceness. Author and philosopher Dallas Willard once wrote that "our most serious failure today is the inability to provide effective practical guidance as to how to live the life of Jesus."[3] I want to give you that guidance in the form of "spiritual disciplines." These are ancient Christian practices we can use to help us grow in our faith. Hopefully we can harness them to prune the idol of niceness and cultivate something better in its place.

As we begin that work, let's keep two things at the forefront of our minds.

The Downward Direction of Spiritual Growth

A few months ago, my husband and I called an arborist and asked him to prune some trees in our yard. The trees were Bradford Pears that had stretched out over our roof and needed to be pulled back. In my mind's eye, I anticipated a few snips here and there, nothing major. When I came home later and saw what the arborists had done, I had to pick my jaw up off the ground. Each tree looked like Shel Silverstein's *Giving Tree* after the boy had taken all its branches. Our pear trees were butchered. The limbs poked off the trunks like nubby spokes. They were so bare they reminded me of a sheep after shearing season.

I was a little embarrassed. We are relatively new to our neighborhood, and I was afraid our street would be angry about the unappealing view. But the next day one of our neighbors was out checking her mail. When she saw the arborist's work, she waved to me, pointed to the trees, and marveled, "That is going to create a *lot* of new growth!"

The more I learn about plants, trees, farming, and flourishing, the more I learn that growth often looks like death. We see this in Matthew 7, when Jesus speaks of cutting down a tree and throwing it into the fire, but we see it elsewhere as well. In John 15:2, Jesus says that God "cuts off every branch in me that bears no fruit, while every branch that does bear fruit he prunes so that it will be even more fruitful" (NIV). And in John 12:24, Jesus teaches, "Unless a kernel of wheat falls to the ground and dies, it remains only a single seed. But if it dies, it produces many seeds" (NIV). In each of these metaphors, Jesus is telling us that there is a phase of growth that doesn't look like growth at all. It looks like loss. It looks like setback. It looks like death.

In nature and in faith, less is often more. It's important to keep that in mind as we think through the work of cultivating. In our culture of "bigger is better," spiritual growth often looks like less. In fact, this is the grand sweep of the Christian life, which culminates in the ultimate example of Jesus's death on a cross. The Christian paradigm for growth is loss. This should empower us to embrace the pain of pruning and even the pain of dying to ourselves. We can do this knowing that a tree pruned by the master only grows more abundantly.

The Spirit Gives the Growth

In 1 Corinthians 3:7, the apostle Paul reflects on his ministry and all that he has invested into others. Looking back on his life and work, he remarks, "Neither the one who plants nor the one who waters is anything, **but only God, who makes things grow**" (NIV, emphasis added). As we turn toward the disciplines and habits of cultivating a better tree, we must always keep in mind that spiritual growth is not something we muster up. It is not a sheer act of will. Instead, it is God who enables our growth.

This is the light burden of Jesus (Matt. 11:30), the knowledge that what God calls us to is hard, and yet it is the Holy Spirit who does the heavy lifting. In addition to that promise, rest assured that God is already at work. He is already doing it. God constantly offers us opportunities to grow, and he is relentlessly going to war against the things that separate us from him. We don't always recognize it because we mistake the pain of pruning as an arrow from the enemy, but sometimes the pain in our lives is God killing the very things that need to die.

Be encouraged in the knowledge that God does not prune us the way I prune plants! He is no amateur cutting and axing and ripping things out of the ground. God knows exactly what needs to be removed in order to help us flourish. We can trust him. So let's roll up our sleeves and dig in.

〰〰〰〰〰〰   TAKING ROOT   〰〰〰〰〰〰

So then, just as you received Christ Jesus as Lord, continue to live your lives in him, rooted and built up in him. (Col. 2:6–7 NIV)

⋀⋀⋀⋀⋀ DIGGING DEEPER ⋀⋀⋀⋀⋀

1. What obstacles to spiritual growth have you encountered?

2. What specific practices have helped you to grow?

3. What has *not* helped you to grow?

4. What habits of niceness do you want to begin pruning out of your life?

9

Grow Original

EMBRACING YOUR DESIGN

Throughout every summer of my childhood, tucked safely behind my grandparents' kitchen counter and away from the hazards of running children, laid rows and rows of homegrown, in-season tomatoes. There were always too many of them to store anywhere else in the house, so there they sat on the blue linoleum floor—dozens of freshly picked tomatoes, still caked with dirt from the ground.

This was an annual tradition of my grandfather's. He loved tomatoes more than any other food, so each year he visited a farmer on the outskirts of Charlotte to collect his quota of fruit. He would return home with his haul and feast on them for weeks.

One of the things I will always remember about my grandfather's tomato-eating habits is that he required the barest amount of seasoning. After slicing open a tomato and displaying it on his plate, he would add just a touch of salt and pepper before cutting into it with a fork. Or he would skip the cutting and seasoning altogether and simply bite into it like an apple.

As a child I didn't like tomatoes, but over the years I matured out of my frozen chicken nugget diet and today I understand why those tomatoes were such a delicacy for him. A good tomato—a truly good tomato—is divinity. Give me bacon, white Wonder bread, rich mayo, and a summer tomato, and I will give you a meal fit for a king.

In fact, one of the best dishes I have ever had featured a medley of heirloom tomatoes. Ike and I were dining at a fancier-than-normal restaurant with elaborate, unknowable menu items like "Duck Pastrami" and "Aged Pecorino." We ordered an appetizer we recognized—bruschetta—and it came to our table with a rainbow of tomatoes cascading across the top. They were gorgeous, but more importantly, they were the most delicious tomatoes either of us had ever tasted. We practically fought over who got to scrape the plate, and we still talk about those tomatoes today. Whenever we eat another *really* good tomato, we look at each other and ask, "Is it as good as those heirlooms?" To which the answer is always, "No, it is not."

That's the funny thing about tomatoes—they can taste wildly different. The tomatoes we ate that night, or the tomatoes my grandfather hoarded like candy, are almost an entirely different fruit from the kind you get on your burger at McDonald's. Not only do fast-food tomatoes have less flavor but they are also harder, less juicy, and more pale.

And there is a reason for that.

Nearly one hundred years ago, a tomato farmer discovered a way to produce the "perfect" tomato. Thanks to a genetic mutation that he was able to reproduce, this farmer created a new breed of tomato known for its "uniform ripening." These tomatoes have an even red color, a symmetrical shape, and extra durability to survive the elements. Uniform ripening improved the attractiveness of the tomato, but along with this "improvement" came one negative consequence—it destroyed the tomato's taste.[1]

Uniform ripening somehow worsened the flavor of the tomato, and for a period of time it was a complete mystery why. But scientists eventually figured it out. What they discovered was a gene responsible for flavor, and the uniform ripening gene disabled the flavor gene. What made the tomato perfect on the outside essentially ruined it on the inside.[2]

This backstory explains the wide spectrum of tomato quality, and the superior taste of heirloom tomatoes. The reason heirloom tomatoes are so much more delicious than their perfectly round counterparts is that they haven't been altered; they are original. Heirlooms develop from a breed of tomato with no imposed genetic mutations. As a result, heirloom tomatoes can appear misshapen and discolored, but their flavor is consistently better.

Farmers altered the original design of tomatoes in order to make them more appealing to buyers, but they degraded the tomato as a result. Niceness does the same. When we alter ourselves in order to be accepted, included, seen, affirmed, or promoted, we not only become inauthentic people but we dull the vibrancy of our original design. We become false people who are

133

spiritually flavorless. In this sense, the story of the tomato is a metaphor for all the ways we falsify ourselves simply to belong.

The Battle to Belong

Throughout this book I have emphasized the ways we use niceness to *get things*. Niceness is a form of social capital we can cash in on in many different ways, and the most obvious form is belonging. We are nice because we don't want to be rejected. We want to be included, accepted, and rewarded, so we put on a façade that can win us that prize.

One of the people who has written most insightfully about this need to belong and the lengths we will go to pursue that goal is C. S. Lewis. In an essay called "The Inner Ring," he shared his own struggle with the need for acceptance. Lewis pointed out that every school, every business, every organization and club possesses an "inner ring" of individuals with extra privilege or special status, and everyone outside it aspires to join. He added that these inner rings are everywhere—from the ivory towers of academia to neighborhoods and churches—and we are slaves to some and blissfully unaware of others.[3]

On some level we all know that the promise of the inner ring is an empty one. It cannot deliver the peace, the confidence, and the belonging we hope it will. But Lewis illuminated exactly why that is: **there are rings inside of rings.** After a great deal of striving and angst, we finally break into an exclusive ring only to discover an even more exclusive ring inside it. Inclusion, then, is never a thing to be grasped. It constantly slips through our fingers like oil.

Another reason why the inner ring is unsatisfying is that **the satisfaction of inclusion does not last.** Lewis writes, "Once the first novelty is worn off, the members of this circle will be no more interesting than your old friends. Why should they be? You were not looking for virtue or kindness or loyalty or humour or learning or wit or any of the things that can really be enjoyed. You merely wanted to be 'in.'"[4]

Lewis said the need to be accepted is "one of the great permanent mainsprings of human action," and if you don't take precautions to guard against it, it will become "one of the chief motives of your life."[5]

I don't think he was overstating this. When I was working on my PhD, I researched the experience of women in work environments dominated by men. In areas like science, math, engineering, technology, and sports, women tend to be significantly outnumbered by men, and I was curious to find out what that was like and how it affected their relationships with other women.

A number of studies noted a shocking dynamic between women that has always stayed with me. Research showed that in some work environments where there are very few women, the women turned *on* each other instead of turning *to* each other.[6] This was exactly the opposite of what I expected. I anticipated a deep level of friendship and connection since they uniquely understood one another. Instead, they were striving to access the inner ring. There was greater competition and further isolation. If a woman complained about being mistreated by her male coworkers—perhaps she was subjected to degrading remarks or even sexual harassment—her female coworkers would distance themselves from her with comments like, "She isn't tough enough to cut it here" or "She needs to stop complaining so much." The subtext of these responses was clear: "I am not like her. I belong here."

For these women, niceness and the ability to get along no matter what were strategies for keeping their jobs and ascending in their careers. It got them something. They had a vested interest in painting on a smile, acting like everything was fine, and condemning the women who refused to do the same. This resulted in women stepping on each other in order to get a leg up in their career, instead of offering one another a helping hand. This everyone-for-themselves mentality also created an environment of toxic inauthenticity. To the people on the inside of the ring, they were one thing; to the people on the outside of the ring, they were something else entirely.

The stories of these women, along with the words of C. S. Lewis, point to the quiet aggression of niceness. As kids, my friends and I used to play a game called king of the hill in which one child stood on top of a hill and tried to knock all the other children off. Whoever was the most effective at fending off their playmates got to stake their claim as king, and in many ways, that is how people go about their lives. Whether it's the best job, the best school, the best neighborhood, or the best clothes, it's tempting to push someone else aside to get it all. Especially if they are rocking the boat, calling out injustice, or challenging the status quo. That's when niceness slithers in smooth and subtle and ready to kill.

- "She just isn't a team player."
- "He is creating division."

- "She simply needs to trust God more."
- "They need to forgive."
- "There is a better way to go about this."

We use our niceness to gently and gingerly *shove* people off the hill, while looking magnanimous in the process. The desire to be accepted and "brought in" to the inner ring is so strong that it cleaves our identities in two. We become disjointed people who look attractive on the outside but are flavorless within. Our "salt has become tasteless" (Matt. 5:13 NASB), not only because our niceness is false but because that falseness impedes our ability to love.

This is, without a doubt, not the way of Jesus, who died on a hill rather than knocked people off of it. But how do we reject the allure of belonging? How do we resist becoming false or competitive? To answer that question, let's look at someone in Scripture who constantly altered himself in order to be accepted, even when he was already accepted by Jesus.

The Disciple Who Craved Acceptance

The apostle Peter is known for a lot in the New Testament, but one of his most famous moments is also one of his worst—his denial of Jesus. Peter's denial was shocking, not only because Peter was one of Jesus's disciples but because of all that Jesus had done for Peter. Jesus saw something in Peter that Peter did not see in himself, and Jesus saw something in Peter that the world did not see in him either. Peter believed he was a fisherman, but Jesus called him to something more, to be a fisher of men (Matt. 4:19). And later on, Jesus would also call Peter to build his church (Matt. 16:18).

In the months and years that followed his initial call, Jesus taught, commissioned, and invited Peter to participate in spectacular miracles. He challenged Peter to be more than he had ever dreamed. Jesus loved Peter and patiently endured with him, even when he was slow to understand or missed the point completely.

Despite all this, Peter was quick to distance himself from Jesus when it became beneficial to do so. Immediately following Jesus's arrest, a servant girl noticed Peter and identified him as Jesus's friend. "This man also was with him," she exclaimed. Peter was desperate to deny his association with Jesus: "Woman, I do not know him." Shortly after that, another individual recognized Peter and asked if he was one of Jesus's followers. Again Peter lied: "Man, I am not." Finally, about an hour later, another person insisted that Peter was one of Jesus's disciples, and Peter once again refuted the truth: "Man, I do not know what you are talking about" (Luke 22:56–60).

At its most basic level, this story is about the fear of man. Peter was afraid, not just of rejection but of arrest and execution. And if we're being honest, who among us can fault him for that? This was a test that he failed, but it was a hard test to be sure.

This story was part of a pattern for Peter. He was a man who desperately needed to be accepted and easily bent to the fear of man. We can see this throughout his life. After Jesus's death and resurrection, Peter became a leading authority in the church, but he continued to struggle with people-pleasing. In Galatians 2,

we read about a confrontation between Paul and Peter, in which
Paul leveled the following accusation against Peter:

> But when [Peter] came to Antioch, I opposed him to his face,
> because he stood condemned. For before certain men came from
> James, he was eating with the Gentiles; but when they came
> he drew back and separated himself, fearing the circumcision
> party. And the rest of the Jews acted hypocritically along with
> him, so that even Barnabas was led astray by their hypocrisy.
> (vv. 11–13)

To understand what is happening here, it helps to know that
there was a group of people in the early church who believed
you had to be circumcised in order to become a Christian.
This group was known as the Judaizers, and they essentially
taught that you must be Jewish in order to follow Christ. Since
Jesus was the fulfillment of Jewish prophecies, the Judaizers
concluded that the Gentiles—non-Jews—had to be grafted in
using the same demarcation that centuries of Jews had used
to set themselves apart.

The apostle Paul, a circumcised Jew, rejected this thinking altogether. In Galatians 3:28, Paul made it clear, "There is neither
Jew nor Gentile, neither slave nor free, nor is there male and
female, for you are all one in Christ Jesus" (NIV). Paul wanted
people to understand that we don't have to *become* anything
in order to come to Christ.

But Peter was afraid of the Judaizers, so he appeased them.
In their absence, he fellowshipped with Gentile Christians, but
when the Judaizers came around, he distanced himself from the
Gentiles in the same way he once distanced himself from Jesus.

Peter was hungry for acceptance. He wanted to be seen, known, affirmed, and celebrated, and this desire drove his choices throughout the course of his ministry. It never seemed fully extinguished, and this aspect of his story is one of the things I truly love about Scripture. It presents us with such utterly human portraits. It would have been so tidy and inspiring if Peter learned his lesson, changed his ways, and never turned back. It would be a great story if, after Jesus's crucifixion, Peter found his courage, overcame his insecurities, and never dealt with them again.

But that is not what happened, because that is not what it is to be human. Each and every one of us will struggle with our old temptations at times. Like Peter, we will always feel the bite of being excluded.

Thankfully we are not left without hope. Or help. In addition to the gift of the Holy Spirit, there are two practical ways we can be authentic and loving instead of altering ourselves and elbowing others in order to be included.

The Discipline of Seeing Yourself Honestly

Niceness is an incredible self-deceiver. It puts on a guise of kindness, even godliness, which is really just a mask for self-interest. That is why the antidote to niceness, and to the overarching idol of acceptance, is not simply the knowledge that we are accepted by God. For some of us that still isn't enough.

That's a truth we learn early in Peter's life, before Jesus's arrest, when Jesus foretold his death and described it in stark terms.

He then began to teach them that the Son of Man must suffer many things and be rejected by the elders, the chief priests and the teachers of the law, and that he must be killed and after three days rise again. (Mark 8:31 NIV)

Rather than ask questions or weep in disbelief, Peter responded rather remarkably. He stood over Jesus and *rebuked him* for his words. Peter responded this way because he did not like what Jesus was saying. It was not at all what Peter had thought he was signing up for. Perhaps Peter imagined a triumphant conqueror who would overcome evil in an impressive demonstration of his power. Or perhaps he expected the Messiah to exalt and vindicate his followers. He did not expect this. Not rejection. Not death. That couldn't be right.

Jesus's reply to Peter was stern and severe: "Get behind me, Satan! . . . You do not have in mind the concerns of God, but merely human concerns" (Mark 8:33 NIV). *Human concerns.* Jesus exposed Peter's true motives. Peter was more concerned with the things that mattered to people than the things that mattered to God.

Jesus's words here are about as harsh as they come, but they gave Peter the gift of seeing himself honestly. What Peter needed to understand about himself was that he was not looking to be accepted by Jesus; Peter was searching for acceptance from others. That is why he never stopped pandering for it. Even the acceptance of Jesus Christ, the Son of God, was not enough.

What's even more devastating—which is evidenced here and later in Peter's denial—is that **Peter wanted acceptance more than he wanted Christ.** This became clear as soon as he had to choose between them.

That's why it is so crucial that we learn to see ourselves through a clear lens. This discipline—which we can also call "the discipline of confession"—is only possible by the power of the Holy Spirit through the illumination of God's Word and the accountability of community. Without these resources, we will deceive ourselves, as Peter did, into believing in a false and superficial form of faithfulness. Peter thought he had a better idea than Jesus of what it meant to be the Son of God. Peter thought Jesus's plan was below his own, so he thought that he was honoring Jesus, dignifying him, and protecting the reputation of the movement, when in reality, Peter was imposing his own skewed understanding of faithfulness onto Christ. This is another way niceness deceives us. It passes off an idolatrous need to be liked as something noble and good. We must practice the discipline of confession, seeing ourselves honestly, and admitting our faults to God, so that we can repent of the falseness that is bearing bad fruit.

Remember how Jesus saw something in Peter that Peter didn't see in himself? God knew what he created Peter for. He knew the plans he had for Peter. He knew how Peter would fail, but he also knew how Peter would rise. The more Peter stepped into that calling, living for the glory of God instead of the praise of man, the more he impacted the world for the better.

When we conform to a narrow mold in order to be included or liked, we reject the plan God has for our lives and shrink our souls in the process. There is a freedom and a purpose in knowing who we are, acknowledging our specific abilities (and inabilities), and using them for the kingdom of God, but we will never experience that fullness if we paper over our God-given design with something generic and pleasing.

That is one of the benefits of tools like personality assessments, which are helpful guides in the journey of understanding who God created us to be. Although these personal insights can become their own rabbit holes and discovering yourself can become an unhealthy end in itself, personality assessments can be extremely useful in the right context. When we use our self-knowledge to build up the church, we can be powerful stewards of whatever God put inside us. As 1 Corinthians 12:7 reminds us, "Now to each one the manifestation of the Spirit is given **for the common good**" (NIV, emphasis added).

We need to ask God to help us see ourselves honestly so that we can be who he created us to be. Not for the sake of some fuzzy notion of self-empowerment but because God designed us for a purpose much bigger than we can imagine—for the health of our souls, the good of the church, and the glory of God.

The Discipline of Secrecy

In a chapter about the fallout of inauthenticity, secrecy may seem like the last thing we should pursue. To understand why this is a spiritual discipline and why it is so effective at pruning the fruit of niceness, let's first recall the basic orientation of niceness.

On its face, niceness seems selfless. It appears to focus on others instead of ourselves, but in reality, niceness is sometimes a gentle way of elbowing our way to the center. It is the socially acceptable way of accessing the "inner ring," while pushing others out in the process. This was what Peter did again and again. He failed to love others as himself because he was so preoccupied with himself.

One antidote to this compulsion in ourselves is to starve the desire to "get" by doing good works in secret. When the desire to be accepted and approved of becomes an idol, it becomes insatiable. Secrecy nails that idol to the cross. In Matthew 6, Jesus suggests, "But when you give to the needy, do not let your left hand know what your right hand is doing, so that your giving may be **in secret**. And your Father who sees in secret will reward you" (vv. 3–4, emphasis added). Then again in verse 6: "But when you pray, go into your room and shut the door and pray to your Father who is **in secret**. And your Father who sees **in secret** will reward you" (emphasis added).

In his book *The Spirit of the Disciplines*, author Dallas Willard calls this the "discipline of secrecy." He describes this discipline as abstaining "from causing our good deeds and qualities to be known."[7] Willard then explains, "To help us lose or tame the hunger for fame, justification, or just the mere attention of others, we will often need the help of grace. But as we practice this discipline, we learn to love to be unknown, even to accept misunderstanding without the loss of our peace, joy, or purpose."[8]

The discipline of secrecy reorients our good works back toward their true destination, which is why Jesus advises us to seek those opportunities out. Look for chances to give without being known or to serve without being thanked.

Thankfully, we don't have to look hard for these kinds of opportunities, because they surround us—every time we are snubbed, ignored, mistreated, or excluded. Every time our niceness is not reciprocated and our sacrifice goes unappreciated. These are the moments when we can become bitter or we can embrace the grace that can only be accessed in secrecy.

In her book *A Beautiful Disaster*, my friend Marlena Graves summarizes this discipline in the loveliest way when she writes: "Being noticed is not our food. The approval of others is not our food. . . . Our food, that which nourishes and makes us whole, is to do God's will."[9] Acceptance cannot promise us that, but quiet obedience lived out for the eyes of Christ alone surely can.

Conforming to Christ instead of the Crowd

One of the fascinating things about heirloom tomatoes is how incredibly different they can look. Some are orange, some are yellow, some are even purple. They come in wildly different shapes with folds and appendages so contorted they seem like defects. And yet they are some of the most flavorful fruits you can find.

I think this is a lovely picture of the many shapes humans take. God made us all so different, and what we often tend to forget—or simply misunderstand—is that our differences reflect the different aspects of God.

Too often we assume the image of God is one single thing, a narrow cookie cutter that each of us must squeeze ourselves into. But that's not at all what being made in the image of God means. In Genesis 1:27, we read this vision: "So God created man in his own image, in the image of God he created him; male and female he created **them**" (emphasis added).

Them. This simple word tells us that the image of God is something we reflect together. Each one of us reflects some aspect of the infinite God. Each one of us embodies some characteristic of our heavenly Father, which means we contribute to an increasingly complete picture of God the more we consider how he is reflected in every person.

We each reflect some part of the image of God that no one else does. Our God-given designs contribute to the richness of that image, so when we hide it or belittle it or are ashamed of it, the image becomes less and less complete. When we embrace who God created us to be, the image is more and more full.

Growing into who God created you to be, becoming the "true you," is not some vague or squishy notion. In *Mere Christianity*, C. S. Lewis offers a different vision of the true self, one shaped not by conformity to the crowd but conformity to Christ.

> Until you have given up your self to Him you will not have a real self. Sameness is to be found most among the most "natural" men, not among those who surrender to Christ. How monotonously alike all the great tyrants and conquerors have been: how gloriously different are the saints.[10]

One might also add, "How monotonously alike all the nice Christians have been." When we conform ourselves to others—even nice Christian people—we inevitably put on something false. But when we conform ourselves to Christ, the more we become our true selves. That is one of the mysteries of our faith—that we can all pursue the same Savior and become more distinctly ourselves in the process. It's as if Jesus is the ultimate salt, who brings out each of our natural flavors.

‿‿‿‿‿ TAKING ROOT ‿‿‿‿‿

For we are his workmanship, created in Christ Jesus for good works, which God prepared beforehand, that we should walk in them. (Eph. 2:10)

‿‿‿‿‿ DIGGING DEEPER ‿‿‿‿‿

1. Can you identify any "inner rings" in your life?
2. Do we ever outgrow the pressure of the inner ring? Why or why not?
3. In your experience, what has helped you to see yourself the most honestly?
4. What are some practical ways you can engage in the discipline of secrecy?
5. We are often told to be ourselves. What do you think is the difference between the world's version of this message and God's?

Grow Deep

ROOTING YOUR SOUL

One afternoon in third grade, I climbed to the top of the monkey bars on my elementary school playground. I laid across them flat on my back and stared up at the sky. The clouds were gray but not particularly ominous. Nothing seemed out of the ordinary, but I had a hunch that was all about to change. The night before I had listened to the weatherman warn about the trajectory of a storm called Hurricane Hugo. I didn't know much about hurricanes—the size or strength or potential for damage—so I gazed up at the sky while my stomach fluttered with excitement.

Several nights later, Hugo slammed into our city. It was a direct hit. In hindsight, I am genuinely shocked at how relaxed my parents were about it, because my dad is the man who plans for *everything*. (He once created a fish habitat behind our lake house "just in case there was an economic depression and we needed to fish for food.") To this day, I have no idea why my parents were so mellow as a non-hypothetical hurricane was bearing down on us, but that's exactly what they were, and I took my cue from them.

The night Hugo arrived, my whole family slept peacefully. I woke to the sound of wind, so I got up from my bed and peered out at the back of the house. The rain was pounding and the trees were swirling, but my swing set was still intact and that was all that mattered. I crawled back into bed, pulled the blanket up under my chin, and went back to sleep.

I looked outside the next morning and couldn't believe my eyes. The sun was out and the wind had calmed, but we were trapped inside our neighborhood. Fallen trees barricaded every road, their trunks much too big for even a band of muscled men to budge. They were thick oaks that the storm had transformed into wrecking balls. One tree crushed an empty car, while others sliced through houses like they were papier-mâché.

At the base of each toppled tree was a wide, elaborate root system sticking straight up into the air. I stepped outside and stood next to one map of tangled roots. It spanned wider than my outstretched arms and must have been twice my height. I marveled that a storm could rip up these roots with the same ease that I could pull a weed. I also wondered why some of these strong trees with thick roots had fallen in the storm, while other seemingly weaker trees had been able to hold their ground.

This random lottery of fallen trees is one difference between a tornado and a hurricane. A tornado's damage is severe but limited, whereas a hurricane is widespread but generally less intense. Some trees fall but many do not and, in that sense, hurricanes have the effect of pruning rather than total destruction.

I decided to do a little research into why some trees fall while others stand, and one of the main reasons I discovered is the quality of the roots. During a strong storm with high winds, a tree's canopy almost functions like the sail of a ship. The wind swoops into the canopy and pushes up against the tree, requiring the roots to serve as an anchor. If the roots are strong, the tree will hold firm; if the roots are weak, the tree will fall.

All sorts of factors can compromise the integrity of the roots. Trees that are located near homes can be especially vulnerable to falling because the construction of the house may have damaged the tree's root system. In urban or rocky areas, where roots can't deepen or spread, the root system becomes precarious as well, but none of this is evident on the surface. A tree can look vibrant and secure up until the moment it is tested by a storm.

In addition to anchoring the tree, roots also strengthen a tree by nourishing it. Roots are the source of nutrients, so when the roots are unable to spread, run into bedrock, or must compete with other trees for food, it stifles the production of fruit.

None of this is detectable to us, but there is one creature that *can* sense a weakened root system, and that is an insect. When a tree is struggling to survive, it emits a heat that bugs can detect. This heat notifies the insects that the tree is vulnerable and open for attack, and in this way, a weakened root system actually sets off a domino effect of destruction.

The relationship between a tree and its roots is a helpful way of thinking about niceness and its fruits. Niceness, like the shallow-rooted tree, looks fine on the surface, but underneath, a gradual weakening occurs. All it takes to expose it is the right storm.

The Shallowness of Niceness

As we have already discussed, niceness is a virtue of "surfaces rather than depths," meaning niceness is inherently shallow. The term *shallow* is usually associated with vanity or obliviousness to the world, but it can also describe a kind of faith that is not rooted in the depths of God and his Word. This kind of faith provides easy answers to hard questions. It has a transactional relationship with God. That is to say, it believes God rewards people who live good lives. One of its primary means of spiritual sustenance is Christian subculture. Shallow faith is bedazzled in Christian jewelry, T-shirts, inspirational signs, and Instagram accounts, but it is not necessarily rooted in the Word of God. That is not to say any of those things are bad or wrong; what matters is the role they play in our faith. If we are more likely to seek truth and encouragement from social media than directly from Scripture, we will become shallow-rooted, undernourished trees bearing bad fruits like cynicism and sentimentality.

Decades after we weathered Hurricane Hugo, the image of those trees is still etched in my mind. It came back to me this year when my family and I moved into a house with skyscraping pine trees just feet from our bedrooms. Almost immediately I informed Ike that we would have to remove them. My hurricane days had me spooked, so we called a tree removal company and started making plans.

Around that same time, I chatted with a neighbor about my past history with hurricanes and how worried I was about our trees. She listened and nodded politely, but when I was done, she pointed to our trees and remarked, "I hear what you are saying, but those pines are unlikely to fall over. Their roots run deep."

The same is true for our lives. Deep roots not only fortify our faith to weather life's storms but also produce better, healthier fruit, fruit that is hopeful without being naïve, passionate without being sentimental, and childlike without being shallow. To understand how to do that, I want to look at one person who modeled this rootedness well—the apostle Paul.

The Apostle Whose Roots Held

As we discussed in chapter 6, Paul was a Jewish man who studied the law and adhered to its every command. In his zeal for God, he spent a number of years persecuting Christians and even overseeing their deaths, but all that changed when Paul encountered Jesus face-to-face. After his resurrection, Jesus appeared to Paul and commanded him to stop persecuting his church. Not surprisingly, this upended Paul's entire life. He became a follower of Christ, one of the very first missionaries, and a founder of the early church. Paul literally changed the world.

After he became a Christian, Paul witnessed miracles and wonders, but he also experienced a lot of pain. Paul was shipwrecked and imprisoned multiple times, and he was betrayed by fellow believers. While awaiting death in prison at the end of his life, Paul learned of rival Christians who rejoiced in his imprisonment. Perhaps they disagreed with some aspect of his teaching or perhaps they didn't appreciate his preaching style, but rather than grieve over the fate of their brother, they added to his torment more. Paul wrote of this in Philippians 1.

> **It is true that some preach Christ out of envy and rivalry,** but others out of goodwill. The latter do so out of love, knowing that I am put here for the defense of the gospel. **The former preach Christ out of selfish ambition, not sincerely, supposing that they can stir up trouble for me while I am in chains.** (vv. 15–17 NIV, emphasis added)

As you read these words, imagine yourself in Paul's situation—alone, uncertain, betrayed by people you thought you could trust—and ask yourself how you would have responded. How would you have felt if you were in his shoes? Would you have been tempted to fall into despair? How many of us would have grown bitter and hard? How many of us would have questioned our entire faith? How many of us would have sworn off church and Christians forever? How many of us would have been tempted to abandon organized religion altogether?

And yet, Paul did none of these things. Paul did not respond with even a hint of anger. Instead he wrote:

> But what does it matter? The important thing is that in every way, whether from false motives or true, **Christ is preached. And because of this I rejoice.** (Phil. 1:18 NIV, emphasis added)

Of all the people who would have been justified in becoming jaded and rejecting the church, it was Paul. This man was hurt by other Christians, and cruelly so, yet his faith remained strong.

What was Paul's secret? In such bleak circumstances, how did he resist cynicism and respond with grace and joy? When we look at his life, we see two biblical perspectives that shaped him.

He Believed What God Said about People

Paul knew and believed what God said about people. I don't mean that God gave him specific information about the people in his life. God is not going to tell you that your Uncle Charles is an indiscreet blabbermouth or that your good friend Mary has an anger problem. When I say that Paul believed what God says about people, I mean that he believed what God's Word says about human nature.

And what God says is complex. On the one hand, we read verses like these:

For all have sinned and fall short of the glory of God. (Rom. 3:23 NIV)

There is no one who does not sin. (2 Chron. 6:36 NIV)

Just as sin came into the world through one man, and death through sin, and so death spread to all men because all sinned. (Rom. 5:12)

All we like sheep have gone astray; we have turned—every one—to his own way. (Isa. 53:6)

None is righteous, no, not one; no one understands; no one seeks for God. All have turned aside; together they have become worthless; no one does good, not even one. (Rom. 3:10–12)

If we say we have no sin, we deceive ourselves, and the truth is not in us. (1 John 1:8)

But on the other hand, God also says this:

So God created man in his own image, in the image of God he created him; male and female he created them. (Gen. 1:27)

God made man in his own image. (Gen. 9:6)

And have put on the new self, which is being renewed in knowledge after the image of its creator. (Col. 3:10)

For you formed my inward parts; you knitted me together in my mother's womb. I praise you, for I am fearfully and wonderfully made. (Ps. 139:13–14)

Are not two sparrows sold for a penny? And not one of them will fall to the ground apart from your Father. . . . Fear not, therefore; you are of more value than many sparrows. (Matt. 10:29, 31)

God paints an incredibly layered and complex portrait of human nature, so if we are going to believe what God says about humanity, we have to hold these seemingly opposing truths together. In the one hand we hold our boundless brokenness, and in the other we hold our identities as image bearers of God. There is not a human on the face of the planet for whom both of these statements is not true, which means our challenge is to uphold them both.

Paul understood this. His perspective on sin was shaped by Scripture, and it guarded him against cynicism. It prevented him from having inflated expectations of people. Paul saw people as they were—as Scripture describes them—which means he was not shocked or undone by sin.

In his well-known devotional *My Utmost for His Highest*, Oswald Chambers explains that this is the secret to guarding against cynicism, especially on the heels of disillusionment. Chambers writes,

> Disillusionment means having no more misconceptions, false impressions, and false judgments in life; it means being free from these deceptions. However, though no longer deceived, our experience of disillusionment may actually leave us cynical and overly critical in our judgment of others. But the disillusionment that comes from God brings us to the point where we see people as they really are, yet without any cynicism or any stinging and bitter criticism.[1]

Paul's understanding of human nature protected him from shattering into cynicism. At the same time, Paul also had hope for people. In the first chapter of Philippians, he practically gushed over his friends in Philippi. But Paul didn't have his head in the sand; he knew what people were capable of. Paul wasn't walking around wearing rose-colored glasses, but he wasn't a pessimist either. He saw people as they truly were, both broken and redeemable. This perspective anchored his faith for the storms of relational brokenness.

He Believed What God Said about Himself

The second perspective that kept Paul's faith rooted was his belief in what God said about himself. Paul knew the Savior he was following. He understood the cost of his faith. He knew what happened to Jesus, he knew why, and he knew what that meant for his own life. Paul realized that his call to follow Jesus meant following the path of Jesus, who loved and sacrificed himself for his people.

Early on, I defined niceness as being pleasing or acceptable in order to get something. Once niceness discovers it isn't getting something in return, it sours fast. The nice Christian becomes shocked and entitled when things don't work out or when circumstances are hard. The temptation, then, is to forget that there is a cross at the center of the gospel.

Paul, however, understood what he was committing to, and it became a source of freedom for him. When he was rejected, abandoned, slandered against, and shamed, Paul rarely seemed surprised. That was exactly what he had signed up for.

Going Deeper

So the question remains: How can we, like Paul, live joyfully without being oblivious to the world? How can we look straight into the darkness without becoming jaded or hopeless? Rather than possess a shallow faith, how can we cultivate something deeper? What are the practical steps we can take? When we look at Paul's life, we see three spiritual disciplines that rooted his faith in the deep soil of God and produced a better fruit.

The Discipline of Study

Ike and I honeymooned on the Caribbean island of Saint Lucia, and it was absolutely dreamy. The beaches were gorgeous, the waters were a thousand shades of blue, and our resort was perched on a mountain. Exhausted from the wedding festivities, I could have laid on the beach all day every day, but my husband, on the other hand, wanted more. The two towering cliffs adjacent to our hotel—the Pitons—plunged deep into the ocean just off the beach. Each spire was nearly eight hundred meters tall, but we were told they extended much farther below the surface. So one day we grabbed some snorkeling gear and swam out. There we discovered a whole other world of beauty. If we had had the capacity to dive deeper, I know we would have encountered even more.

That difference—between the beauty of the shore and the beauty of the depths—reminds me of Scripture. So often we approach God's Word a bit like the water that laps up on the beach. These shallow waves are gorgeous and blue and might even give us a glimpse of some colorful fish darting around. Yet this sparkling water—as breathtaking as it is—is nothing compared to the majesty of the ocean beyond. The reefs, the dolphins, the turtles, the thousand shades of blue—there is so much to explore, but we will never reach it if we are satisfied to sit on the beach.

We live in a culture that is content to swim around in the shallow end of God's Word. We have our arsenal of verses that we enlist for the hard situations in life, but we don't always explore the breadth or depth of Scripture. As a result, we sometimes talk about Scripture with the authority of an oceanographer who has never actually left the shore.

Some of us, however, have been to the deep end. We swam in it for a while. We know all about the depths of the ocean.

But we haven't been back in ages. We are sailors docked in port whose knowledge about the ocean is stagnant and stale.

These habits are so easy to fall into in our sound-bite society. We have a list of verses we love, but we don't always know their context or how they connect to the rest of God's Word. Using Scripture this way is sufficient when life is good, but it falters in times of suffering. Shallow faith cannot prepare us for the mysterious brokenness of life. Shallow faith, and a shallow knowledge of God's Word, also lead us to give shallow answers to people who are suffering. It is a superficial knowledge of Scripture and of God that tells a grieving mother, "Everything happens for a reason."

For all these reasons and more, we need to equip ourselves with the knowledge of God's Word. That doesn't mean we each need a master's level education to understand the Bible—Jesus's own disciples were uneducated men—but it does mean we should never stop learning, studying, and listening. Not so we can puff ourselves up but because God has given us an ocean of himself to explore and discover, both for our good and for the good of the world.

Paul understood this. He knew Scripture inside and out. It shaped his view of God and of others. It prepared him to engage the world's complexity with the breadth and depth of an infinite God. It protected him from cynicism, directed him when he was disoriented, and rescued him from despair. It also gave him implausible joy and peace. It provided him with hope in circumstances when he could have been tempted to despair. Paul did not pursue knowledge for knowledge's sake or to win an argument with a rival but in order to know his beloved Jesus and to persevere until he would one day be reunited with him.

The Discipline of Worship

The second practice that rooted Paul's faith deep into the ground was worship. We see this all throughout the book of Philippians, when Paul sat in prison awaiting his fate while at the same time exhorting his friends to rejoice. We also see this discipline exemplified in Acts 16, when Paul and Silas sing hymns to God while they sit together in chains.

In many ways worship is the application of study. It is taking what we learn about God and speaking it over our circumstances, declaring what is true. It was Mary's response of faith when she discovered she was pregnant with Jesus (see Luke 1:38) and Job's response when he lost everything he had (see Job 1:20). As both of these examples demonstrate, worship is a discipline since it does not always reflect how we feel. Sometimes we would rather do anything but worship.

However, in those moments when we worship in spite of how we feel, it's a bit like sipping broth when we are sick. We might not be hungry but our bodies need nutrients in order to heal, so we force down some ginger ale and chicken noodle soup, knowing it's what our bodies need. In some seasons of life, worship is like that. Even when it is an act of plain obedience, worship nourishes and restores our souls. Paul didn't worship in spite of his circumstances; he worshiped in order to survive them.

The Discipline of Hope

The final practice that enabled Paul to root himself in Christ was the discipline of hope. We don't often think of hope as a discipline, but much like the other fruits we have studied, it is a virtue we cultivate. We do the work, and God provides the growth.

The kind of hope that is sturdy and rugged is not the same as idealism or wishing. Karen Swallow Prior sorts out these differences by clarifying that there is a kind of hope "common to all human experience," which is a "sense of anticipation for a future outcome."[2] This sort of hope—hoping to go out on a date this weekend, hoping to get a promotion at work—takes no discipline at all. It is more like a human reflex.

Likewise, we must not confuse the discipline of hope with blind optimism. Prior writes, "Hope is not the same as oblivion or naiveté. Hope requires reckoning with the world as it is, with reality."[3]

In contrast with superficial idealism, the discipline of hope—*Christian* hope—is rooted in something more substantive than a wish and more reliable than optimism about the world. It is rooted in the ability and character of God. This sort of confidence springs from our repeated and willful decision to surrender and trust ourselves to Christ.

Throughout Paul's letters, we see this discipline in action. The word *hope* appears nearly fifty times, and its reference point is always Christ. This habit is the reason Paul is able to suffer persecution, shipwrecks, imprisonment, and abandonment, and still sing out God's praises. His hope was never rooted in his circumstances. It was never rooted in the inherent goodness of human nature. And it was never rooted in the presumption that "things would work out in the end." Instead, Paul continually directed his gaze toward the source of all hope. He spoke of it again and again, and through this habit of focus, God provided the fruit.

Rooted in Christ

In John 15:5–8, Jesus once again draws on the metaphor of a tree to teach us about growing in him.

> I am the vine; you are the branches. If you remain in me and I in you, you will bear much fruit; apart from me you can do nothing. If you do not remain in me, you are like a branch that is thrown away and withers; such branches are picked up, thrown into the fire and burned. If you remain in me and my words remain in you, ask whatever you wish, and it will be done for you. This is to my Father's glory, that you bear much fruit, showing yourselves to be my disciples. (NIV)

The disciplines of study, worship, and hope are a part of that abiding work. These are practical steps we can take to root ourselves to the vine that bears much fruit.

There is, however, an important difference between us and the oak trees that collapsed during Hurricane Hugo. There is also a difference between us and the pine trees that withstood the storm. For both the oak and the pine, their ability to survive and flourish depends on their ability to hold. For those of us in Christ, we are already being held.

When we anchor our roots in Christ, his roots grow in us. When we remain in the vine, the vine remains in us. It is almost like a set of invisible hands is anchoring us through the battering of the wind and the rain. This Jesus who was never cynical, this Jesus who was never sentimental, this Jesus who did not plug his ears and ignore the sin, this Jesus who did not look away from brokenness and think happy thoughts instead, this Jesus who is the very definition of depth—he accomplishes what niceness never will. When we are rooted in him, our roots hold, not because we have such a firm grip on him but because he has such a firm grip on us.

〰〰〰〰 TAKING ROOT 〰〰〰〰

Blessed is the man who trusts in the LORD, whose trust is the LORD. He is like a tree planted by water, that sends out its roots by the stream, and does not fear when heat comes, for its leaves remain green, and is not anxious in the year of drought, for it does not cease to bear fruit. (Jer. 17:7–8)

〰〰〰〰 DIGGING DEEPER 〰〰〰〰

1. What are the characteristics of shallow faith?
2. What do you think keeps you in the shallow end of faith? What prevents you from going deeper?
3. Proof texting is the practice of taking a Bible verse out of context and using it to prove your point. Why is this practice so tempting, and what do you think are the consequences of it?
4. What are some easy first steps to practicing the discipline of study?
5. We often think of worship as the songs we sing on Sunday. How does it shift in your mind to describe it as a discipline?

Grow Less

PRUNING YOUR PRODUCE

"You might lose people."

Throughout my years as a writer and a teacher, I have periodically fielded this warning from good-hearted, well-intentioned people who wanted me to steward my influence well. The caution, usually delivered with tenderness and care, still cut me to the core, because I have long been driven by a need to achieve. I want to make an impact. I want to be taken seriously. I want people to listen to me. What I do not want to do is lose people.

This desire is in most of us. In one way or another, we all wrestle with the fragile nature of influence. The parent who wants to dispense advice without alienating his child. The twenty-something who wants to share her concerns about her friend's dating relationship but doesn't want to hurt or alienate the friendship. The daughter who wants to confront her mother's prejudice without straining the relationship. The pastor who wants to hold a church member accountable—a member who is also one of the congregation's biggest donors. We all want influence—and sometimes we want it for good and noble things—but because of this, we will go to extreme lengths to preserve it.

One of the most common tools for influence is the "social lubricant" of niceness. It avoids hard conversations and difficult truths at any cost, for the sake of maintaining a relationship. And because of that, niceness rarely "loses people." Instead it aims to keep them all.

The Idolatry of Fruit

Earlier this year my family moved into a new house, and one of the first things I noticed in the yard was a crape myrtle with a large branch splitting off from the side. Crape myrtles, if you have never seen one, do not look like stereotypical trees. In place of a single trunk is a collection of stems, almost like a dinner fork sticking out of the ground. Its bark is smooth, light, and peels off like paper. The foliage erupts out of the top like a feather duster, and it blossoms into pink during the summer and spring.

For the longest time, I could not figure out why one tree branch had cleaved off the side, but I assumed one of our boys had something to do with it. Knowing them, I assumed they had attempted to swing on the branch and snapped it in the process, so I left it at that.

Months later I discovered the true cause of the break. It was a summer day and the tree was in full bloom when a storm swept through. The tree withstood the wind and the rain without any effort at all, but afterward the branches drooped nearly to the ground. After studying the tree I realized the raindrops were weighing down the flowers and the leaves, and the tree was struggling to bear up under the extra weight.

As I stared at the tree and its sagging limbs, suddenly it all clicked. I figured out why that one branch had broken off. In all likelihood, it had collapsed from the load of its own blooms.

In our culture we tend to view all growth as good growth and all fruit as good fruit. This message guides our ministries and our faith, and because of it, we are tempted to do whatever it takes to get results. There are entire industries and markets driven by this conviction, but this measure of goodness and richness is not how God designed the world. When we look at his creation, "more" is not always "best."

In peach trees, for example, more fruit can actually become a problem. When a peach tree produces too many peaches, the resulting fruit is of a lower quality. The peaches are small, hard, and generally underdeveloped, because the tree's nutrients are finite. A large amount of produce stretches the tree's resources too thin. As one gardening site explains, "When branches are overloaded, each fruit receives a smaller share. There's simply not enough water and nutrition to go around. The result is small fruit with hard, moistureless flesh."[1]

In addition to producing a lower quality of fruit, an overabundance of it impacts the overall health of the tree: "Overloaded branches will sap the tree's resources and weaken it, making it more susceptible to disease and decreasing its lifespan."[2]

Because of these two consequences, peach farmers "thin"—a form of pruning—their trees to ensure that a smaller number of fruit receive a greater amount of nutrients. This can be accomplished by plucking the blossoms so that the peaches are spaced about six to eight inches apart. The thinning can also happen on a larger scale by cutting away the tall branches and shaping the tree into a wide bowl.[3]

What this tells us about both trees and human beings is that God did not design us to be infinite producers. "More" is not always better—for trees or for souls—which means "influence" is not our greatest asset. Influence can be a wonderful good in the hands of God, but it can also become an idol in its own right, a master we serve at the cost of obedience.

Niceness is one of our preferred manners of serving this idol. We want to increase our influence, but we don't want to alienate people. This can make us two-faced or cowardly. We don't want to say a hard thing, or a true thing, for fear of "losing people." This threat hangs over us like a guillotine blade, waiting to chop off our effectiveness.

That said, it can be difficult to recognize the idolatry of fruit, because we disguise it in such holy terms.

- "I am doing it for the kingdom."
- "I don't want to needlessly push people away from Jesus."
- "Why distract people from the gospel?"

Each one of these sentiments carries a kernel of wisdom. We should indeed avoid petty jabs, unhelpful oversimplifications, and mean-spirited generalizations. No matter how hard the message or how searing the truth, we are not excused from kindness, gentleness, love, and self-control. As the French essayist Joseph Joubert once put it, "Never cut what you can untie."[4]

Influence and success can be wonderful tools, but they must never become ends in themselves. When the fruit of our ministries becomes the be-all and end-all, it's tempting to sacrifice integrity, godliness, honor, and courage in order to get results, as if the ends always justify the means. It's also tempting to bend to fear and insecurity and baptize it as wisdom.

Sometimes the fear of "losing people" is just a prettied up idolatry of influence, veiled in spiritual language to hide its true allegiance to power, control, and self. When we look to God's Word, we see a very different approach.

The Prophet Who "Lost" People

Ezekiel was a prophet with an especially tough calling. He lived at a time when God's people openly rebelled against him, and because of this, Jerusalem fell to an invading nation. It was a dark chapter in Israel's history, and this was the mess into which God called Ezekiel. In chapter 3, God issued the following instructions to his prophet:

> Go now to the people of Israel and speak my words to them. You are not being sent to a people of obscure speech and strange language, but to the people of Israel—not to many peoples of obscure speech and strange language, whose words you cannot understand. Surely if I had sent you to them, they would have listened to you. But **the people of Israel are not willing**

to listen to you because they are not willing to listen to me, for all the Israelites are hardened and obstinate. (vv. 4–7 NIV, emphasis added)

It was a strange mission that did not make much sense, because God had already doomed it to fail. God dispatched Ezekiel to a people who would not listen to him. He even clarified that their inability to listen had nothing to do with Ezekiel's talent or ability. If God had sent Ezekiel to another land, the people would have received his words and repented. But that was not the job. Instead, God sent Ezekiel to his own people, an obstinate people, who were unwilling to listen to what he had to say.

In a sense, he was commissioning Ezekiel to fail.

God concluded his instructions with this command: "Go now to your people in exile and speak to them. Say to them, 'This is what the Sovereign LORD says,' whether they listen or fail to listen" (Ezek. 3:11 NIV).

Had I been Ezekiel, I would have been confused. Why go if the people are not going to listen? Why waste my breath?

But in sending Ezekiel, God redefined "success." Old Testament scholar Iain Duguid puts it this way:

What do the models of Jesus and Ezekiel tell us about our efforts in evangelism and missions? In the first place, surely they challenge the common notion in the church that "bigger is always better." There is a lot of pressure from many quarters in our times to measure success in terms of numbers. Whether it is evangelistic crusades that speak of thousands of "decisions for Christ" or popular books that suggest adopting certain methodologies will inevitably bring church growth, the "bigger is better" philosophy reigns in much of the contemporary church.[5]

Coincidentally, Duguid then draws on the same language of fruit that we have been exploring here.

> It is asserted on the one hand that the faithful Christian will inevitably be the fruitful Christian, seeing many people brought to Christ, and on the other hand, that fruitfulness should determine strategy, so that the maximum number of harvesters are sent to where the fruit is ripe. . . . The call of Ezekiel (and some of the other prophets) should challenge this simplistic assumption.[6]

What we can learn from Ezekiel and others like him is that **sometimes the call isn't to succeed but to obey.** Sometimes obedience is success. Sometimes the call is not to bear the fruit but to prune the branches. Sometimes the call is to lose people.

The Discipline of Obedience

In the face of confrontation or conflict, niceness offers an enticing escape. Rather than speak a hard truth that could alienate our family or friends, it's tempting to focus on the things we agree on. But the story of Ezekiel pushes back on this, and more importantly, so does Christ. Jesus didn't simply "lose people." His message was so offensive that it got him killed. Following him does not require us to seek out or instigate strife for its own sake, but it does mean we will encounter it and that we should not flee.

This is the spiritual discipline of obedience, and through it, God thins the bad fruit and even the good fruit in order to cultivate the best. That said, I want to offer three practical examples of obedience that specifically target the idols of influence in our lives.

Speak to Your People

These days, whenever I hear the warning "You might lose people," a part of me wants to ask, "Which people? Poor people? Scared people? Hurting people? Lonely people? Or do you mean *my* people?"

Many of us nice Christians are willing to speak the truth in love so long as we are speaking it to other people "out there." We will criticize that other group, that other strand of Christianity, those other people outside the walls of our church. This allows us to call ourselves bold while maintaining our nice Christian image because we never turn the critical eye on our own group.

In contrast, notice something important about Ezekiel's story. Ezekiel went to *his* people, the people of Israel. God did not send him to people in a foreign land. God sent him to his own community, and that is how we die to influence. That is how we die to the idolatry of fruit. We do it through our willingness to say what is true to the people who love us most, even when it's hard or controversial.

This may mean talking to a family member whose drinking seems to be out of control. This may mean challenging a friend who has been flirting with someone who isn't their spouse. And this may mean holding our church leaders accountable for some form of abuse.

When we faithfully speak the things that are true, even when it's hard, we not only guard the integrity of our community but we thin the trees of our souls and do the hard, long-term work of bearing better fruit.

Harden Your Forehead

Some of us overcorrect our niceness by swinging in the opposite direction: communicating our thoughts and opinions in a way that is belittling, judgmental, or just plain mean. Ironically those of us with this struggle—which isn't nice at all—are just as enslaved to the idol of influence as anyone else. We simply attract different people who are also angry, anxious, or disaffected.

God, on the other hand, had a different approach. When he spoke to Ezekiel about the people of Israel, he described the hardness of their hearts, and he challenged Ezekiel to be even harder, but in a completely different way. "I will make you as unyielding and hardened as they are. I will make your forehead like the hardest stone, harder than flint" (Ezek. 3:8–9 NIV). Notice that God does not tell Ezekiel to harden his heart in response to the rigidity of the Israelites. Instead he tells Ezekiel to harden his *forehead*. This distinction makes all the difference in the world, because it is the difference between longevity and burnout, between love and despair. Throughout the Bible, hardness of heart primarily describes a person's orientation toward God, so whenever we harden our hearts—to whomever and for whatever reason—there is a sense in which this is also a hardening of ourselves toward God. And we cannot flourish that way.

Our foreheads are another matter. We can harden our foreheads while maintaining a heart that is soft toward God and his children, and that is the place out of which we can speak truth well. It equips us to lead with fortitude and determination rather than condescension or contempt.

Of course this takes practice. When I was in middle school, I joined my first soccer team and learned a skill called "heading the ball." A soccer player is allowed to direct the ball using their forehead, which enables them to maneuver the ball in ways that their feet cannot. But I tell you what, I hated this move. At first it hurt like the dickens. I dreaded the practices with drill after drill of whacking the ball with my head.

My dislike for this move was cemented when, during a game, two players kicked the ball at the same time and it flew like a missile toward my face. I tried to head the ball, but the ball headed me instead. It knocked me clear off my feet and onto the ground, temporarily blinding me. I will never forget lying there on my back while the referee ran to my side, knelt down, and asked, "Are you seeing stars?"

"I can't see *anything*!" I whimpered.

A few minutes later, my sight returned, but it left me disoriented and afraid. From that day on, I was even more intimidated by our practices, but my coach pushed me to keep going.

I never did like heading the ball, but my forehead toughened over time. I no longer flinched before my skin made contact, and it no longer left my head spinning. Instead I became comfortable enough with the move to use it when the game required.

Hardening our foreheads to speak the truth in love is a lot like that process. Sometimes the blowback from our words will knock us straight off our feet and leave us reeling for awhile. Those of us who are used to being nice, being liked all the time, and reaping the benefits of our likability have soft foreheads. Confrontation—even necessary, clear-cut, biblical confrontation—is disorienting and scary. But the more we learn to do it, the more we will learn to do it well. Our foreheads will become increasingly like flint.

And our hearts? We will find them increasingly pruned to make way for better fruit.

Say Yes to the Silly and the Small

About a year ago, God called my husband to do something kind of weird. At the time, we had sensed God leading us to plant a church in a very particular area, but we didn't have a specific location in mind. Other pastors had warned us we would have trouble finding a space in the area where we were looking, and they were exactly right. Although it is one of the fastest growing areas in the nation, it is short on locations suitable for a church. So we did the only three things we could: we searched, we fasted, and we prayed.

One day, in the middle of this process of discernment, Ike felt a sudden urge to drive to the mall—which sat in the center of the area where we were looking—and walk around it. Plain, simple, and out of the ordinary. So he got out of his car in the middle of the summer and the dead heat of the day and started to circle the building. He felt silly doing it. He was wearing boots and hipster skinny jeans as he tromped through the grass and traced the perimeter of the property. But he believed the Spirit had led him there, so he listened and obeyed. He walked the entire circumference of the mall—probably about the distance of a mile.

For months Ike felt God drawing him back to that place. At least once a month, in the middle of the day and especially at times when we were confused or scared, Ike would sense the pull of God inviting him to go and walk with him. And so he did, again and again.

When Ike would go out to the mall to meet with God, I was reminded of the Israelites circling the walls of Jericho, waiting for the walls to come down. I wondered what walls God was preparing to crumble in our town. What strongholds would he overcome?

And then the first wall came down. The movie theater in that mall—the movie theater that had said no to us eight months prior, the movie theater that had said no to every other church plant before us, the movie theater that was in the very center of the location where God had commissioned us—said yes. They wanted us to launch our church out of their location.

I don't know what would have happened if Ike had chosen to say no to the silliness of walking the perimeter of the mall. I don't know if our story would have ended any differently. But if you ask Ike he will tell you that God met him there. When Ike said yes to walking and sweating and praying, he experienced holy encounters with the living God, and that is what we learned from that journey: the value of obeying in the small things but also in the seemingly silly.

Not all acts of obedience are like Ezekiel's. Obedience is not always dramatic, grand, or even dignifying. Sometimes obedience can feel downright humiliating. But those small opportunities to obey—whether it is silly and strange or just the ordinary habits of reading the Bible and praying each day—are forming us into the kind of people who are not only fortified to obey when it's hard but also to discern the voice of the Shepherd from the bleating of sheep.

The Savior Who "Lost" People

Jesus was loving but he was not nice, nor was he a slave to worldly influence. If anything, he was the opposite. Rather than fall all over himself using palatable language or trying to be clear, he spoke in intentionally opaque parables. Rather than sweet-talk the religious power brokers, he called them "vipers" and "whitewashed tombs" (Matt. 23:27, 33). Rather than use his access to political leaders for the benefit of himself and his followers, he kept a clear allegiance to the Father. And rather than maintain a superficial unity with his disciples, he rebuked them and challenged them with truth.

All this from the most influential man who ever lived.

Of course this does not give us free reign to say whatever we want and let the chips fall where they may. Jesus rebuked people for whom he would also die on a cross. He offended people, but his ultimate desire was to save them. We must hold together the fullness of his witness.

The starting point for obedience, then, is not always found in questions like "What message am I called to share?" or "What do I need to accomplish for God?" but instead "What is derailing my own faithfulness?" "What do I need to *thin*?"

"Which idol is shaping my message and my life more than Christ?" Maybe it's an idolatry of results or an addiction to success. Maybe it's a worldly notion of influence or a false belief that the ends always justify the means. Maybe it's an idol of control. Whatever is inhibiting your faithfulness to the character and message of Jesus, take a step in the direction of thinning the fruit, pruning the branches, and casting it into the fire. It may not make sense to everyone and we may even lose people along the way, but we can do all of these things when we remember that Jesus did them first and it changed the entire world.

TAKING ROOT

I am the true vine, and my Father is the gardener. He cuts off every branch in me that bears no fruit, while every branch that does bear fruit he prunes so that it will be even more fruitful. (John 15:1–2 NIV)

DIGGING DEEPER

1. In which areas of your life do you have the greatest amount of influence?
2. Where do you see the "idolatry of influence" in your community or in your church? What specific forms do you see it taking?
3. Why do you think God called Ezekiel to a mission that would, from a worldly perspective, fail?

4. What is the difference between the world's definition of success and God's definition of success?

5. What are practical ways you can engage in the "discipline of obedience"?

Grow Wild

FLOURISHING IN THE WILDERNESS

Shortly after my first son was born, I developed a strange, intense fear of him falling. I lay partial blame on the giant open stairwell in the middle of our home. At that time, we were living in a house with an unconventional floor plan. About two yards past the threshold of our front door was a gaping ten-foot drop. A waist-high bannister wrapped around the space, but that provided me no comfort at all. We had to pass by the stairwell whenever we crossed from one part of the house to another, and I was convinced this layout spelled catastrophe. What if Ike was walking by the stairwell and tripped? What if our son tumbled out of his arms and into the hole? I would literally lie awake at night imagining these scenarios in my brain.

One morning I woke up and decided I would no longer subject myself to this harrowing risk. I would do something about this peril. I would take control of my life! And so I did. My dad and brother were in town, so I sent them to Home Depot with one assignment: purchase a large net and some zip ties. We would use both to cover the hole.

The plan did not unfold like I hoped. For starters, Home Depot was fresh out of baby-catching nets, so we settled for a volleyball net instead. It had neon-yellow plastic around the edges, making it a hard-to-miss eyesore in the center of our foyer. Then we faced the obstacle of securing the net to the wall. We were able to anchor two of the edges to the bannister, but the remaining two were a challenge. Short of drilling into the drywall of a house we didn't own, we did not have many options. Eventually we settled on adhesive Command hooks, which were not terribly strong but were sturdy enough to slow a falling baby. That was my logic anyway.

It probably goes without saying that my husband hated this net. He thought it was both ugly and weird. Everyone in my family teased me about it, and our visitors were consistently bewildered. The whole contraption was so over-the-top that it was patently ridiculous.

Not surprisingly, that net never did see action. It sat uselessly in our home as a flimsy, neon-yellow shrine to my fear. To this day, the image of that net cluttering our home while providing no real added security exists in my memory as a symbol of the ways we slavishly serve our fears. Our devotion to safety and security knows almost no bounds—no matter how absurd!—and this isn't limited to our physical security. We also yearn for comfort in our relationships and in our faith, and niceness is an effective means for maintaining both. But it comes with a cost.

A Hothouse Faith

I already picked on tomatoes in chapter 9, but I am going to single them out one more time, because there is something else we can learn from them. There are a lot of reasons some tomatoes are watery and tasteless, and we have already looked at a big one—alterations to their original design. But there is another reason some are bland. Tomatoes grown in greenhouses, or "hothouses," are also notorious for their bad taste. The balmy growing conditions of hothouses make it possible to eat tomatoes all year round, but we pay for this access with quality. Although the tomatoes are cultivated in a sheltered environment, safe from adverse weather conditions, pests, and diseases, the controlled conditions worsen their flavor. These hothouse tomatoes are only a muted version of the tomatoes grown in the wilderness.

Scientists have been trying to figure out why hothouse tomatoes taste so different from those grown in the wild, and one factor they discovered was the absence of ultraviolet light. The glass walls of hothouses filter out the UV light of the sun, and this missing component has been linked to an alteration in the tomatoes' flavor.[1] To try and remedy this, researchers compared the taste of tomatoes grown in hothouses with UV light to tomatoes grown in a hothouse without UV light. There was a noticeable improvement; however, both still fell short of tomatoes grown outdoors, which suggests that UV light is not the only factor.

I wonder if you are noticing a pattern here. Whether it is perfecting the tomato's appearance or controlling the tomato's environment, these "improvements" are not improving much at all. Bigger is not always better, more is not always best, and what we learn from the hothouse is that security does not produce success. Instead, some plants and trees flourish as a direct result of trial and loss.

This principle is written all over creation. When we look at nature, we discover that danger, damage, and unpredictable elements can actually *contribute* to the health and well-being of a tree, because these factors have a way of pruning the things that need to be taken away.

This principle also holds true for our souls, though everything in us resists it. Everything in us wants to protect ourselves, plan ahead, cover every base, control every element, avoid all controversy, and anoint all our idols of security as "wisdom."

When we do this with niceness—hemming ourselves in from conflict, confrontation, or the simplest disagreement—it's as if we are erecting balmy hothouses in which our faith can grow. These environments are safe from a good deal of adversity and hard things, but the fruit it produces is bland. These "hothouse fruits" of a secure and sheltered faith are barely worth eating at all.

The bland produce of the hothouse is one reason why we intentionally step out of it by taking risks and saying bold things, but the more important reason is this: it's what Jesus did. Rather than stay safe at the right hand of the Father, rather than keep the peace by getting along with the Pharisees, rather than preserve his life and defend himself to Pilate, Jesus exposed himself to our wild and broken world. As his followers, our calling is the same.

However, Jesus was not the only person in the Bible who rejected the comforts of a hothouse life. Moses left his palace and fled into the wilderness. Daniel was tossed into a lions' den. Shadrach, Meshach, and Abednego chose to be thrown into the fire. And in addition to these brave men, the Bible describes Esther, a brave woman who could have remained in her comfortable world by playing along and being nice but instead chose to follow a higher calling.

The Queen Who Was Not Nice

The story of Esther began a lot like the fairy tale of Cinderella, only if Prince Charming was named Xerxes and he was a horrible jerk. We first met Xerxes, king of Israel, after a weeklong party during which "each guest was allowed to drink with no restrictions" (1:8 NIV). Everyone in the palace had been drunk for days, and in that state, Xerxes summoned his wife, Queen Vashti, to come and "display her beauty to the people and nobles, for she was lovely to look at" (1:11 NIV). He wanted to show off Queen Vashti like a trophy, his most prized accessory, his nice, beautiful wife.

But Vashti wasn't having it. This woman had moxie. Instead of obeying the king, Vashti rebuffed him. She denied his request, remained in her quarters, and left him to stew in his rage. In return, Xerxes banished her from his presence—which, if we're being honest, is a little like breaking up with someone who has already dumped you. In doing so, Xerxes made an example of Vashti; this was the fate of independent, opinionated, not-nice women who defied the king.

Shortly after, the king launched a search for Vashti's replacement by issuing a decree: "Let a search be made for beautiful young virgins for the king" (2:2 NIV). The king's attendants gathered up as many lovely women as they could find, and from that group, the king would choose his next queen.

Meanwhile, a Jewish orphan named Esther was living outside the palace gates with her cousin, Mordecai, who had taken her in as his own daughter. Esther "had a lovely figure and was beautiful" (2:7 NIV), and because of this, she was chosen to join King Xerxes's harem. Esther caught Xerxes's eye and began to receive special attention. In keeping with Mordecai's instruction, Esther withheld the truth of her family background, and she continued to ascend in favor. After a year of grooming and preparation, Xerxes chose Esther as his queen.

Over and over again, the book of Esther describes the strength of Xerxes's attraction to Esther. She was exactly what he was looking for, the perfect replacement for his rebellious former wife. But this is where the story takes a surprising turn.

One of the king's advisors, a man named Haman, resented the Jewish inhabitants of the kingdom, and he began to conspire against them: "There is a certain people dispersed among the peoples in all the provinces of your kingdom who keep themselves separate. Their customs are different from those of all other people, and they do not obey the king's laws; it is not in the king's best interest to tolerate them. If it pleases the king, let a decree be issued to destroy them" (3:8–9 NIV). Xerxes agreed and permitted Haman to do as he pleased.

When Esther heard this terrible news, she had a choice to make: protect her spot as "queen of the hill" or lay herself down upon it. She knew what happened to her predecessor, Vashti, who had broken with protocol and stepped out of her place. She knew what happened to women who refused to be seen and not heard, who raised their voices and pushed back against the powers that be. She also knew the law of the land: anyone who approached the king without being summoned was to be put to death.

As Esther deliberated, Mordecai spoke words of courage and conviction into her heart: "Do not think that because you are in the king's house you alone of all the Jews will escape. For if you remain silent at this time, relief and deliverance for the Jews will arise from another place, but you and your father's family will perish. And **who knows but that you have come to your royal position for such a time as this?**" (4:13–14 NIV, emphasis added).

Esther had a choice to make. She could choose between being nice, staying in her place, and stepping on others in order to be safe, or she could leverage her privilege and risk her life for people "outside the gate" of power.

Esther considered her choices and determined what she had to do: "I will go to the king, even though it is against the law. And if I perish, I perish" (4:16 NIV).

So Esther went. After three days of praying and fasting, she approached the king, asked him to spare her people, and he agreed. Esther, and her people, were saved.

Cultivating Courage

Karen Swallow Prior writes that "courage requires putting a greater good before a lesser good."[2] This definition is incredibly helpful, because we often think of courage in terms of "right and wrong," which oversimplifies the work of courage. In reality, situations that demand courage are not that black and white. When we back down from taking a risk or stepping out in faith, it is often *for a very good reason*. Esther had a good reason to stay silent—namely, preserving her life. She didn't want to die; no one could fault her for that. Similarly, the moments when we reject courage are very often for our own good or for the good of our families. When we choose what is best for us, it is not necessarily wrong. But it is not courage.

That's the challenge. If we want to be people of courage, the question is not "How do we discern right from wrong?" Although that is an important question, instead we need to ask, "How do we become the kind of people who place the higher good above the lower good?" That is a lot easier said than done.

When we look at Esther's life, we see a woman who could have retreated into the "hothouse" of the palace and lived a safe and sheltered life. She was certainly tempted to, but instead, she exposed herself to risk and chose a higher good over a lesser good. But she didn't do this out of the blue. Courage is not something we wake up and choose; it's something we are formed into, and in Esther's life, we see four disciplines that cultivated her courage.

The Discipline of Confession

We discussed this discipline in chapter 9, but it bears repeating. Confession is not simply about admitting our sin but seeing ourselves honestly and **admitting our need for God**. When it comes to courage, confession often comes down to admitting we are afraid.

This is precisely what Esther does. Advocating for the Jews was not Esther's idea; it was Mordecai's, and Esther wasn't wild about it. When Mordecai first asked Esther to defend her people, she reminded him of the stakes—she would be risking her own life for others. She wanted to make sure he understood exactly what he was asking of her.

When we practice the discipline of confession, when we say out loud that we are afraid, it is the first step to overcoming a stronghold in our lives, because fear has a way of silently dictating our decisions. When we identify a fear and admit it, we reduce its power over us.

This is why God repeatedly commands: "Do not fear." He is naming a stronghold in some part of our lives that he wants to claim as his own. Our fears work hard to protect our idols, and we will not surrender them until we name them. By doing so, we also confess our resistance to courage and invite God to work in a way we had not allowed him to before.

The Discipline of Prayer

Once Esther made the decision to defend her people, she asked them to fast and pray for three days. Again this reminds us that an essential precursor to true courage is acknowledging our weaknesses and our inability to be courageous on our own. Whether we are on the cusp of a big decision or we want to become more courageous people in our everyday lives, we can ask God to walk alongside us in our troubles. By the power of the Holy Spirit, we can ask him to form our hearts and souls and minds so that we are able to discern between the lower good and the higher good. That leads us to another kind of prayer that is just as important, if not more so: asking God to search us so that he can expose the fear inside. Sometimes we are so good at hiding our fear that we don't even recognize it in ourselves. Instead we call it stewardship or "being practical." We need the help of the Holy Spirit to discern when our niceness, our peacemaking, and our control are really just masks for fear.

The Discipline of Listening

There is a crucial moment in the exchange between Mordecai and Esther that I don't want you to miss. In chapter 4, Esther protests, "I have not been called." In response, Mordecai essentially tells her, "Your privilege, your position, is your calling" (see vv. 11–13).

That short interaction is a whole sermon in itself—the ways we passively abdicate responsibility and make our obedience conditional—but for now I will simply point to the boldness of Mordecai's charge and Esther's willingness to hear him. If Mordecai had not said something, Esther may not have approached the king at all. She needed voices in her life who would challenge her to show courage and steward her influence well. This aspect of Esther's story reminds us how important it is to surround ourselves with friends, family, and mentors who will instill us with courage and conviction.

Unfortunately some communities do just the opposite. They perpetuate niceness in order to keep the peace, or they passively discourage us from being brave by feeding into the status quo and inviting us to do the same. If we want to be people of courage, then we must seek out friends who are also pursuing courage and radical obedience to Christ. Faith and trust are so much easier to cultivate when we don't feel like we are doing it alone.

The Discipline of Suffering

Courage does not develop in a vacuum. We do not wake up one morning, after a lifetime of self-protection and bowing to fear, fully formed as people of resolve. Instead, courage is cultivated through a regular habit of performing small acts of bravery and having a willingness to face hard things.

The story of Esther hints at this pattern of courage. Before she confronted Xerxes about the Jews, Esther had a history of stewarding her influence. She shrewdly kept her full identity a secret, and she even reported an assassination plot to the king (2:22). All along the way, she dismissed the temptations to self-indulge and self-protect, using her position to cultivate her inner fortitude instead.

Courage, then, is not to be stored on the shelf until we are ready to use it. Esther's ability to say a giant yes to God could not have been born out of a lifetime of noes. Courage is a muscle we can only strengthen with use, and this truth can cast a new light on the things we fear. In the same way that tomatoes are richer for the harsh elements they endure, we can receive the slings and arrows of life as part of our preparation. They are teaching us to walk in courage, and they are enriching our witness in the process.

Regardless of fear or pain or discomfort, nothing is too small to be transformed or redeemed, if we only have the eyes to see it. We can either flee from situations that are hard or we can embrace them on the journey.

That is how we will become people of courage—one step at a time. Niceness may not seem like the greatest barrier to our courage, but if courage (and character!) is cultivated by way of habits—those daily opportunities we either squander or seize—then niceness is the choice we make in one direction or another.

The question we have to ask ourselves is whether we trust God. Do we trust him to use the things that scare us, even hurt us? Can we trust him with our lives—with our children's lives, with our friends' lives—in this frightening, broken world? And if we decide to trust God, what would that look like? How would our lives look different from everyone else's? These are the questions courage demands of us. But more importantly, these are the possibilities that the resurrected Jesus Christ invites us to dream.

 TAKING ROOT

We rejoice in our sufferings, knowing that suffering produces endurance, and endurance produces character, and character produces hope, and hope does not put us to shame, because God's love has been poured into our hearts through the Holy Spirit who has been given to us. (Rom. 5:3–5)

DIGGING DEEPER

1. Looking back, how has God used the hard things in your life to grow you?

2. If we can see God's faithfulness in the past, that he has used our trials for our good, why do we still fear them and run from them?

3. Where do you tend to seek comfort and security apart from Christ?

4. Who are the people who speak courage and conviction into your life?

5. How would your life look different from others if you were to trust God with the things that scare you?

13

The Fruit That Lasts

About two hundred years after Jesus lived, a twenty-one-year-old woman named Perpetua converted to Christianity and was thrown into prison for her faith.[1] Perpetua was a Roman aristocrat who lived in Carthage—modern-day Tunisia—at a time when Christians were heavily persecuted.[2] Despite this persecution, the gospel was spreading throughout all levels of society, both the ruling classes and the poor, and Perpetua joined the movement.[3] She was all in.

Eventually Perpetua's Christian faith was discovered, so she forfeited her position of privilege, was thrown into prison with her newborn child, and awaited her execution. There she was joined by a Christian slave named Felicity, who was pregnant and equally unwilling to deny her faith.

While the two women awaited their sentences, Perpetua's father visited her, begging her to recant her faith. For the sake of her life and the future of her child, he pleaded with her to turn from Jesus. But Perpetua refused. Her allegiance was to Christ alone. She would not deny her Savior.

Shortly after, Perpetua and Felicity marched to their deaths with their heads held high. An eyewitness describes the women and their fellow martyrs as unflinching in their resolve: "The day of their victory dawned, and they proceeded from the prison to the amphitheater, as if they were on their way to heaven, with gay and gracious looks; trembling, if at all, not with fear but with joy."[4] Perpetua reportedly entered the arena singing a "psalm of triumph,"[5] and one historian wrote, "It had been anticipated that the Christians would beg and plead for mercy. Instead, they defiantly passed before the jeering crowd and presiding Roman procurator."[6]

In the centuries following, the diary Perpetua kept has become a Christian classic of sorts. It has inspired and emboldened generations of Christians who marvel at her courage and her sacrifice. That was the effect it had on me. I first read Perpetua's words when I was in seminary and not much older than she at the time she was persecuted. At roughly twenty-three years old, I was ready to take on the world. I was stunned and exhilarated by the testimonies of Perpetua and Felicity, and I told their story often. I shared it with other young women like myself. I thought their witness could be a rallying cry for our generation.

Years later, as a wife and a mom, I read their story and I only feel sobered. The details of their deaths, which are as gruesome as they are inspiring, are difficult to fathom. I struggle to wrap my mind around the difficult choice they made—staying true to Jesus or staying alive for their newborn children—and I feel incredibly humbled. To be perfectly honest, there are days when I look at Christian leaders and wonder, "Are they following the same Jesus I am?" But then I read stories of martyrs like Perpetua and Felicity and I have to ask, "Am I following the same Jesus as *they are*?"

After all, Perpetua and Felicity were literally mauled by wild animals for the sake of Christ, while I cave at the threat of mean comments on my blog.

A Better Vision

The story of Perpetua and Felicity is so dramatic and overwhelming that it is difficult even to connect with it. It's tempting to dismiss their story with a breezy "I could never do that," but I sincerely hope that you won't. I want you to know I am sharing their story for two reasons.

The first is that these two young women are what I envision when I say, "God never called us to be nice." With these words, I do not envision screaming or name-calling or debating online. I do not envision rants or outrage or self-righteousness. I envision these women and disciples like them. Perpetua and Felicity were not nice Christian women. They did not stay within the lines. They did not submit to authorities who told them they must recant or die. Perpetua did not walk the path marked out for her by her family or her station, but instead she lowered herself and gave it all away. Both of these women counted the cost. To paraphrase the words of Jesus in Matthew 13, they sold everything they had to buy the field, knowing a greater treasure was buried inside it.

Perpetua and Felicity bear witness to a kind of discipleship that is so much deeper and total than the nice Christianity that has come to define our generation. They were loving, kind, patient, and long-suffering, but they were also bold, brave, and did not back down. That quality of faith, not the false obedience that pervades the church today, is what we are called to.

This faith is also our heritage. Do not for one moment forget that Christians like Perpetua and Felicity are our spiritual ancestors. Do not allow your vision to be shaped, or your imagination to be dulled, by the pervasiveness of shiny, easy faith. Do not accept the religion or cause that slaps Jesus on as a label while panting after power, privilege, and self. This lip service to Jesus, this shallow palatable faith, is everywhere, which makes it seem acceptable, normal, and even faithful, but hear me when I say *it is not*.

This nice Christianity is not where we came from and it is not who we are called to be. Remember your Savior, remember your baptism into his death and resurrection, and remember that we are the heirs to a long line of disciples who spit on the idols of their day to pursue a higher, better call. Do not forget them. Do not normalize lukewarm faith.

Remember.

The second reason I am sharing their story is this: Perpetua and Felicity's story testifies to **the higher impact of sacrifice over nice.** What made their story powerful was not their great personalities. It was not how nice they were to everyone, or that they were really great listeners. The reason Perpetua and Felicity's story has endured is what they were willing to lose in order to gain Christ.

Nearly two thousand years later, I wonder if we have replaced sacrifice with enslavement to nice. I wonder if niceness has become a shortcut for bypassing the hard things that give our witness its actual weight. I wonder if we believe that all we have to do is be really, really, *really* nice or likable or avoid words that alienate people, and *that* will be the thing that compels people to become followers of Jesus.

In 1 Corinthians 9:22, Paul describes his strategy of becoming "all things to all people," in order to win them to Christ, which means our language and rhetoric matter. We should pick our words carefully and never intend to offend. But, *but*, let's be clear about what gives us our credibility, because it is not our niceness, in whatever form that takes. If anything, niceness becomes a boundary limiting what we can or cannot say. The authority of niceness evaporates as soon as we say something that people don't like. What we need is an authority we can leverage to say loving things but also hard things. That kind of authority comes through sacrifice.

When we look at the cross and all the martyrs that follow, we see that nothing amplifies our words and establishes our authority more than the megaphone of sacrifice. People will listen to just about anything we have to say if they know we would give up everything for it.

What I Hope You Take from This Book

For several years now, I have wrestled with the gap between Perpetua's and Felicity's faith and my own. I have wrestled with the gap between the Western church and the early church. And most of all, I have wrestled with the gap between who we are and who we are called to be. Although I have been in ministry for quite a while, I found myself revisiting questions I thought I had settled long ago, questions like:

- How do we disciple people who live truly courageous lives?
- How do we disciple people who rise above the culture of constant outrage?
- How do we disciple people who transcend the worldly lines of division?
- How do we disciple people who are willing to obey God when it costs them?
- How do we disciple people who truly love God and truly love others ahead of themselves?

In short, how can we be who we say we are?

As I have processed these questions, I believe there are many different ways to answer them, but one option, one *tree* I have come to realize we must cut down, is the habit of niceness. This habit is convenient for our careers, our relationships, and our reputations, which is why it is such a common fixture of our everyday lives. It's more common than other habits like study, worship, confession, and obedience, but because it is our habit of choice, it has cultivated something shallow and frail where the character of Christ was meant to be.

All of that to say, I hope it is clear that this book is about so much more than people-pleasing. It's about the false formation that has replaced conformity to Christ. It's about the elegant idolatry that has quietly inched itself onto the throne of our hearts. It's about being who we say we are and who God called us to be. If that is our aim, then we need to name the bad fruit, cut down the tree, pull out the roots, and adopt the habits that will actually bear the fruit of Christ through the power of his Spirit.

◊ ◊ ◊ ◊ ◊ ◊ ◊

When I look at Perpetua and Felicity, I feel a bit like a tiny seed staring up at a giant oak. The distance between my faith and theirs seems insurmountable. What heartens me, however, is remembering that I have the same tools and the same Holy Spirit that they had available to them. The same steps that grew the saplings of their faith are available to grow mine, and they're available to grow yours too.

It is also helpful to remember that Perpetua and Felicity probably didn't feel like pillars of faith. As they sat there in that prison, Perpetua's father begging her to recant, her baby crying in her arms, I wonder if they felt small and weak. I wonder if they felt like their lives were just beginning, only to be buried in the ground. I wonder if they felt less like oaks and more like seeds.

We will never know what truly transpired in the hearts and minds of those two young women, but I suspect they both had moments of fear, weakness, and doubt because Jesus did too (see Matt. 26:36–46). When I look closer at Perpetua and Felicity, two Christians who were not "nice" but were obedient to the end, I see humans like myself. I see *exactly* what God can do with men and women like me, because the faith of Perpetua and

Felicity was never about them but the power of the Savior they served. This Savior, this God, created a world in which a kernel of wheat that dies in the ground can produce an overflowing harvest of fruit. Which means God doesn't need any of us to be an oak. Just a seed that sows itself in him.

ACKNOWLEDGMENTS

As I look back on the year I spent writing this book, one phrase comes to mind: "It takes a village to raise a child." This project really did take a village. If not for the wide network of supportive friends and family making sacrifices of time, energy, childcare, and cooked meals, I would not have been able to bring this book into the world. In the span of time I wrote these words, I gave birth to our third child, our family moved, and we planted a church—none of which created an ideal writing environment! Suffice it to say I could not have written this book without help.

First and foremost, I want to thank my parents, Rich and Debbie Hodde, who moved heaven and earth to make themselves available to our kids, all because they believe in me and the call God has placed on my life. Mom and Dad, I can never thank you enough for the many ways you serve our family and love our kids. It is an incalculable gift. In addition to that, I would not be the woman I am, or have accomplished what I have accomplished, without your sacrificial love and generosity.

In addition to my parents, my mother-in-law, Ellen Miller, is a wonderful source of support. Ellen, you are a woman I truly esteem, I love to spend time with, and I trust implicitly with our children. I cannot express how grateful I am to have you in my life.

I owe a huge debt of gratitude to Brooke Robotti, who not only babysat our kids but became an extension of our family along the way. You went above and beyond the call of duty to make time for me to write, and I absolutely would not have finished this book in a timely manner without your help!

Thank you to Baker—and specifically Rebekah Guzman—for patiently giving me extra time to work on this book. I realize not all authors enjoy the grace and understanding that was extended to me as I wrote ever so slowly amid a mountain of other commitments, and I cannot thank Baker enough. Your whole team has supported me as a writer, but more importantly, as a person. And thank you also to Nicci Hubert for stepping in as my editor and helping this book to be the best it can be.

Thank you to Jana Burson, my incomparable agent, who continues to be a source of wisdom and encouragement in my work and in my life. I have grown as a writer and minister of the gospel because you push me to be more, and I would not be where I am today without your guidance and expertise.

Thank you to Christina Edmondson, Hannah Anderson, and Lore Wilbert for serving as sounding boards while I processed these ideas. Each of you supplied me with deep, biblical insight at just the right time. This book is stronger because you generously shared your time and attention with me.

Thank you to *Mere Orthodoxy* and *Christianity Today* for allowing me to use excerpts from articles I wrote for their sites.

The editors for each of these sites sharpened my thinking as God prepared my heart and my mind for this book.

Thank you to my three treasures—Isaac, Coen, and Sadie—who are a constant source of joy in my life. I hope you will read these words one day and know how deeply I delight in you. My love for each of you grows by the day. Our house was loud and hectic in this season while I wrote a book and we planted a church, but you three managed to lighten the load. You made us laugh at just the right times, and you also reminded us of what mattered most. I will never stop thanking God for how he designed each one of you and the richness you have added to our lives. I am hopelessly smitten with each of you.

A falling-all-over-myself THANK YOU to my husband, Ike, who is my teammate, my best friend, and my inspiration. In many ways, your character is the embodiment of this book. You are a man of tremendous strength and iron-spined conviction, but you are also gentle, kind, patient, and compassionate—qualities that run so much deeper than "nice." I learn from you every day—about Jesus, about God's Word, and about myself—and I am so humbled to be loved by you. Thank you for believing in me and challenging me to use my gifts in areas that stretch me. I love you so much. You are one of God's most extravagant gifts to me.

And finally, most of all, thank you, Jesus. Thank you for embodying this message so perfectly and lifting our eyes to a higher, better way. Thank you for giving me the courage and conviction to write these words. Thank you for calling us to something so much better than the safe and comfortable lives we would choose for ourselves. And most of all, thank you for YOU. Thank you for giving yourself to us, because you are the prize, you make life worth living, and you give us infinitely more freedom, meaning, purpose, and peace than "niceness" ever could.

NOTES

Introduction

1. Tim Keller, *Counterfeit Gods: The Empty Promises of Money, Sex, and Power, and the Only Hope That Matters* (New York: Penguin Books, 2011), xvii.

Chapter 1 The Fruit of Niceness

1. Dictionary.com, s.v., "nice (*adj.*)," accessed January 28, 2019, http://www.dictionary.com/browse/nice.

2. Carrie Tirado Bramen, *American Niceness: A Cultural History* (Boston: Harvard University Press, 2017), 10.

3. Bramen, *American Niceness*, 10.

4. Bramen, *American Niceness*, 11.

5. Evelyn Sommers, *The Tyranny of Niceness: Unmasking the Need for Approval* (Tonawanda, NY: Dundurn Press, 2005), 21.

6. Plato, "Meno" in *The Dialogues of Plato, Volume 1*, trans. B. Jowett (New York: Random House, 1920), 356.

7. Bramen, *American Niceness*, 30.

8. Philip G. Ryken as quoted in an endorsement of Barry H. Corey's *Love Kindness: Discover the Power of a Forgotten Christian Virtue* (Carol Stream, IL: Tyndale, 2016), v.

9. Bramen, *American Niceness*, 9.

10. Miroslav Volf as quoted in an endorsement of Barry H. Corey's *Love Kindness: Discover the Power of a Forgotten Christian Virtue* (Carol Stream, IL: Tyndale, 2016), i.

11. Sommers, *Tyranny of Niceness*, 29.

12. Karen Swallow Prior, *On Reading Well: Finding the Good Life through Great Books* (Grand Rapids: Brazos Press, 2018), 23.

13. Randy Alcorn, *The Grace and Truth Paradox: Responding with Christlike Balance* (Colorado Springs: Multnomah, 2003), 73.

14. Alcorn, *Grace and Truth Paradox*, 77.

Chapter 2 Fake

1. Andy Crouch, "Stonewashed Worship," *Christianity Today*, April 12, 2006, http://www.christianitytoday.com/ct/2005/february/23.82.html.

2. Howard Schultz, *Pour Your Heart Into It: How Starbucks Built a Company One Cup at a Time* (New York: Hachette, 1997), 248.

3. Crouch, "Stonewashed Worship."

4. Brennan Manning, *The Ragamuffin Gospel: Good News for the Bedraggled, Beat-Up, and Burnt Out* (Colorado Springs: Multnomah, 2005), 126.

5. Carl Wilson, "Why Do We Love Bad Singing?" *Slate*, August 12, 2016, http://www.slate.com/articles/arts/music_box/2016/08/florence_foster_jenkins_and_the_history_of_bad_singing.html.

6. Karen Swallow Prior, *On Reading Well*, 207.

7. Barry H. Corey, *Love Kindness: Discover the Power of a Forgotten Christian Virtue* (Carol Stream, IL: Tyndale, 2016), xx.

8. Corey, *Love Kindness*, xiv.

9. Emily Freeman, "An Invitation to Rediscover Kindness," *Emily P. Freeman Blog*, March 31, 2016, http://emilypfreeman.com/love-kindness/.

10. Philip G. Ryken as quoted in an endorsement of Barry H. Corey's *Love Kindness: Discover the Power of a Forgotten Christian Virtue* (Carol Stream, IL: Tyndale, 2016).

11. Evelyn Sommers, *Tyranny of Niceness*, 32.

12. Corey, *Love Kindness*, xiv.

13. Sommers, *Tyranny of Niceness*, 36.

14. Sommers, *Tyranny of Niceness*, 21.

15. Sommers, *Tyranny of Niceness*, 29.

16. Sommers, *Tyranny of Niceness*, 30.

17. Megan Hill, "Keeping It Real: The Truth About Authenticity," *Christianity Today*, September 2012, https://www.christianitytoday.com/women/2012/september/keeping-it-real-truth-about-authenticity.html.

Chapter 3 Rotten

1. Sue Carlton, "Douglas Cone, Road Magnate at Center of Scandal, Dies at 86," *Tampa Bay Times*, December 2, 2014, http://www.tampabay.com/news/douglas-cone-road-magnate-at-center-of-scandal-dies-at-86/2208574.

2. ABC News, "Tampa Man Apparently Had Two Families," September 6, 2003, https://abcnews.go.com/GMA/story?id=124800&page=1.

3. Carlton, "Douglas Cone."

4. ABC News, "Tampa Man."

5. ABC News, "Tampa Man."

6. Alanna Vagianos, "She Was the First Woman to Go Public About Nassar. Read Her Statement in Full," *Huffington Post*, January 24, 2018, https:// www.huffingtonpost.com/entry/rachael-denhollander-nassar-impact-state ment_us_5a690ef6e4b0e563007627aa.

7. Tracy Connor and Sarah Fitzpatrick, "Gymnastics Scandal: 8 Times Larry Nassar Could Have Been Stopped," *NBC News*, January 25, 2018, https://www.nbcnews.com/news/us-news/gymnastics-scandal-8-times-larry -nassar-could-have-been-stopped-n841091.

8. Connor and Fitzpatrick, "Gymnastics Scandal."

9. Brendan McDermid, "Victim of Ex-USA Gymnastics Doctor Says Abuse Led to Dad's Suicide," *Reuters*, January 16, 2018, https://www.reuters .com/article/us-gymnastics-usa-nassar/victim-of-ex-usa-gymnastics-doctor -says-abuse-led-to-dads-suicide-idUSKBN1F52MS.

10. Oxford Living Dictionary, s.v., "shrewd (*adj.*)," accessed February 6, 2019, https://en.oxforddictionaries.com/definition/us/shrewd.

11. Carrie Tirado Bramen, *American Niceness*, 9.

12. Dietrich Bonhoeffer, *The Cost of Discipleship* (New York: Touchstone, 1995), 43.

Chapter 4 Bland

1. "Say What You Want to Say," *Vimeo*, posted by Matt and Oz, March 30, 2015, originally aired on *Saturday Night Live* in March 2015, https:// vimeo.com/123645581.

2. Thomas Aquinas, *Summa Theologica*, I-II, q. 23, aa. 8, http://www .newadvent.org/summa/3023.htm.

3. C. S. Lewis, *Screwtape Letters* (2015; repr., New York: HarperOne, 1996), 16–17.

4. Lewis, *Screwtape Letters*, 17.

5. Randy Alcorn, *Happiness* (Carol Stream, IL: Tyndale, 2015), 71.

6. Bruce Waltke, *A Commentary on Micah* (Grand Rapids: Eerdmans, 2007), 111.

7. Waltke, *Commentary on Micah*, 125.

8. Walter Brueggemann, *The Creative Word: Canon as a Model for Biblical Education* (Philadelphia: Fortress Press, 1982).

9. The preceding four paragraphs originally appeared in an article I wrote for *Propel* titled "A Call for Prophetic Leaders," December 2016, http://www .propelwomen.org/content/a-call-for-prophetic-leaders/gjeb5p.

10. This paragraph originally appeared in an article I wrote for *Mere Orthodoxy* titled "Evangelicalism and the Loss of Prophetic Imagination," February 9, 2017, https://mereorthodoxy.com/evangelicals-loss-prophetic -imagination/.

11. Paul Coughlin, *No More Christian Nice Guy* (Minneapolis: Bethany House, 2016), 17.

12. Martin Luther King Jr., "Letter from Birmingham Jail," April 16, 1963.

Chapter 5 Bitter

1. William Desmond, *Cynics* (New York: Routledge, 2008), 2.
2. Desmond, *Cynics*, 2.
3. Paul Coughlin, *No More Christian Nice Guy*, 119.
4. Paul E. Miller, *A Praying Life: Connecting with God in a Distracting World* (Colorado Springs: Navpress, 2009), 80.
5. Miller, *A Praying Life*, 66.
6. Andrew Byers, *Faith Without Illusions: Following Jesus as a Cynic-Saint* (Downers Grove, IL: Intervarsity, 2012), 7.
7. Miller, *A Praying Life*, 77.
8. C. S. Lewis, *God in the Dock* (Grand Rapids: Eerdmans, 2014), 118.

Chapter 6 Hard

1. Tim Keller, "The War Between Your Selves (Part 1)," *Gospel In Life*, August 17, 1997, https://gospelinlife.com/downloads/war-between-your-selves-part-41/.
2. Flannery O'Connor, *Wise Blood: A Novel* (New York: Farrar, Straus and Giroux, 2007), 16.
3. Though not confirmed, this quote is often attributed to author Corrie ten Boom.

Chapter 7 Processed

1. Douglas Todd, "Sentimentality: The Dark Side," *Vancouver Sun*, January 28, 2012, https://vancouversun.com/news/staff-blogs/the-dark-side-of-sentimentality.
2. Benjamin Myers, "The Sentimentality Trap," *First Things*, November 2016, https://www.firstthings.com/article/2016/11/the-sentimentality-trap.
3. Myers, "The Sentimentality Trap."
4. Matt Reagan, "Seven Sentimental Lies You Might Believe," *Desiring God*, November 27, 2015, https://www.desiringgod.org/articles/seven-sentimental-lies-you-might-believe.
5. W. B. Yeats as quoted in Douglas Todd, "Sentimentality: The Dark Side," *Vancouver Sun*, January 28, 2012, https://vancouversun.com/news/staff-blogs/the-dark-side-of-sentimentality.
6. Joni Eareckson Tada, *A Place of Healing: Wrestling with the Mysteries of Suffering, Pain, and God* (Colorado Springs: David C. Cook, 2010), 30–31.
7. Tada, *A Place of Healing*, 31.
8. John Piper, *A Hunger for God: Desiring God Through Fasting and Prayer* (Wheaton: Crossway, 1997), 14.
9. Steven Jillson, "Sentimentality and God's Name," *Darn Sermons* (blog), February 11, 2015, http://darnsermons.com/sentimentality-gods-name/.
10. Michael Lipka, "Why America's 'Nones' Left Religion," *Pew Research Center*, August 24, 2016, http://www.pewresearch.org/fact-tank/2016/08/24/why-americas-nones-left-religion-behind//.

Chapter 8 Cultivating a Better Tree

1. Richard Sterling as quoted in Joseph Stromberg, "Why Does the Durian Fruit Smell So Terrible?" *Ask Smithsonian*, November 30, 2012, https://www.smithsonianmag.com/science-nature/why-does-the-durian-fruit-smell-so-terrible-149205532/.

2. Joseph Stromberg, "Why Does the Durian Fruit Smell So Terrible?" *Ask Smithsonian*, November 30, 2012, https://www.smithsonianmag.com/science-nature/why-does-the-durian-fruit-smell-so-terrible-149205532/.

3. Dallas Willard, *The Spirit of the Disciplines: Understanding How God Changes Lives* (New York: HarperOne, 1999), 110.

Chapter 9 Grow Original

1. Dan Charles, "How the Taste of Tomatoes Went Bad (And Kept On Going)," *All Things Considered,* NPR, June 28, 2012, https://www.npr.org/sections/thesalt/2012/06/28/155917345/how-the-taste-of-tomatoes-went-bad-and-kept-on-going.

2. Charles, "Taste of Tomatoes."

3. C. S. Lewis, "The Inner Ring," *C. S. Lewis Society of California*, http://www.lewissociety.org/innerring/.

4. Lewis, "The Inner Ring."

5. Lewis, "The Inner Ring."

6. Erin Whiteside and Marie Hardin, "'I Don't Feel Like I'm Up Against a Wall of Men': Negotiating Difference, Identity and the Glass Ceiling in Sports Information," *Journal of Intercollegiate Sport* 4, no. 2, (December 2011): 210–26.

7. Dallas Willard, *Spirit of the Disciplines*, 172.

8. Willard, *Spirit of the Disciplines*, 172.

9. Marlena Graves, *A Beautiful Disaster: Finding Hope in the Midst of Brokenness* (Grand Rapids: Brazos Press, 2014), 134.

10. C. S. Lewis, *Mere Christianity* (New York: HarperCollins, 2001), 226.

Chapter 10 Grow Deep

1. Oswald Chambers, *My Utmost for His Highest* (Uhrichsville, OH: Discovery House, 2017).

2. Karen Swallow Prior, *On Reading Well*, 124.

3. Prior, *On Reading Well*, 129.

Chapter 11 Grow Less

1. Jackie Rhoades, "Peach Tree Thinning—How and When to Thin a Peach Tree," *Gardening Know How*, last modified April 5, 2018, https://www.gardeningknowhow.com/edible/fruits/peach/peach-tree-thinning.htm.

2. Rhoades, "Peach Tree Thinning."

3. Rhoades, "Peach Tree Thinning."

4. Joseph Joubert, *Some of the "Thoughts" of Joseph Joubert*, trans. George Calvert (Boston: William V Spencer, 1867), 86.

5. Iain Duguid, *The NIV Application Commentary: Ezekiel* (Grand Rapids: Zondervan, 1999), 73.

6. Duguid, *NIV Application Commentary*, 73.

Chapter 12 Grow Wild

1. Joshua Krisch, "Scientists Discover Why Most Tomatoes Taste Awful—And How to Fix It," *Vocativ*, September 21, 2016, https://www.vocativ.com/360793/greenhouse-tomatoes/index.html.

2. Karen Swallow Prior, *On Reading Well*, 90.

Chapter 13 The Fruit That Lasts

1. William Farina, *Perpetua of Carthage: Portrait of a Third-Century Martyr* (Jefferson, NC: McFarland, 2008), 2.

2. Farina, *Perpetua of Carthage*, 2.

3. Farina, *Perpetua of Carthage*, 3.

4. E. C. E. Owen, *Some Authentic Acts of Early Martyrs* (Oxford: Clarendon Press, 1927), 89.

5. Owen, *Acts of Early Martyrs*, 89.

6. Farina, *Perpetua of Carthage*, 16.

ABOUT THE AUTHOR

Sharon Hodde Miller leads Bright City Church in Durham, North Carolina, with her husband, Ike. In addition to speaking all over the country and earning her PhD, she is the author of *Free of Me: Why Life Is Better When It's Not about You*. Sharon is a regular contributor to sites like She Reads Truth, Propel, and *Christianity Today*, and she has blogged at SheWorships .com for over ten years. When she is not leading, teaching, or writing, her favorite place to be is at home with her husband and three kids.

Connect with
Sharon!

To learn more about Sharon's
writing and speaking, visit

SheWorships.com

 SharonHoddeMiller   SHoddeMiller   SharonHMiller

LIKE THIS
BOOK?
Consider sharing it with others!

- Share or mention the book on your social media platforms. Use the hashtag **#NiceBook**.

- Write a book review on your blog or on a retailer site.

- Pick up a copy for friends, family, or anyone who you think would enjoy and be challenged by its message!

- Share this message on FACEBOOK:
  I loved #NiceBook by @SharonHoddeMiller // @ReadBakerBooks

- Share this message on TWITTER:
  I loved #NiceBook by @SHoddeMiller // @ReadBakerBooks

- Share this message on INSTAGRAM:
  I loved #NiceBook by @SharonHMiller// @ReadBakerBooks

- Recommend this book for your church, workplace, book club, or class.

- Follow Baker Books on social media and tell us what you like.

f ReadBakerBooks **🐦** ReadBakerBooks **📷** ReadBakerBooks